232

6/86 (ABC)
(Que)

THE LEGACY OF JESUS

THE LEGACY OF JESUS

JOHN MACARTHUR, JR.

4291

MOODY PRESS

CHICAGO

All Scripture quotations, except those noted otherwise, are from the *New American Standard Bible*, © 1960, 1962, 1963, 1968, 1971, 1972, 1973, 1975, and 1977 by The Lockman Foundation, and are used by permission.

Scripture quotations marked KJV are from the King James Version of the Bible.

The following chapters were originally printed as booklets by Dr. Mac-Arthur and have been revised for this edition: chapter 1, "The Humility of Love"; chapter 2, "Unmasking the Betrayer"; chapter 3, "The Marks of the Committed Christian"; chapter 4, "The Solution to a Troubled Heart"; chapter 5, "Jesus Is God"; chapter 6, "The Coming of the Comforter"; chapter 7, "The Gift of Peace"; all © 1983 by John F. MacArthur, Jr.; and chapter 8, "What Jesus' Death Meant to Him"; chapter 9, "The Vine and the Branches"; chapter 10, "Abiding in Christ"; all © 1984 by John F. Mac-Arthur, Jr.

Library of Congress Cataloging in Publication Data

MacArthur, John F.
   The legacy of Jesus.

   1. Bible.   N.T.   John XIII-XV — Criticism, interpretation, etc.   2. Jesus Christ — Teachings.   3. Christian
life — 1960-   I. Title.
BS2615.2.M28   1986   232.9′58   85-26023
ISBN 0-8024-8254-3 (pbk.)

1 2 3 4 5 6 7 Printing/LC/Year 88 87 86

Printed in the United States of America

Contents

Introduction

Without question, some of the most poignant, powerful teaching in all of Jesus' earthly ministry took place on the last evening He spent with His disciples before He was crucified. The occasion was the Passover meal, and it has come to be known as the Last Supper. *The Legacy of Jesus* examines Jesus' teaching in those awesome hours the night He was betrayed.

Before the meal was over, Jesus would institute the Lord's Supper. From that point on, believers would not commemorate lambs' blood on doorposts; they would commemorate the Lamb of God slain on the cross once and forever. It was a momentous transition — the New Testament age was beginning. No longer would men remember Passover lambs in Egypt. They would remember that slain Lamb, Jesus Christ, and not just once a year but all the time.

During that meal, Jesus explained the legacy He would leave behind when He departed from this world to go to the Father. His words were intimate, personal, and full of love for those He called His own. And the message has meaning across the ages for us. The promises He made, the legacy He left, are ours to claim. I advise you to devour it. Consume it. Savor every word of it. It is Jesus reiterating to you how much He loves you.

My prayer in offering this book is that those who know Jesus Christ will grow in their understanding of the riches that are ours because of His love for us, and that those who do not know Him will be convicted of their need to surrender completely to Him as Lord and Savior.

As we study these chapters together, may the Spirit of God impress on each of our hearts the importance of giving our all to Him who freely gave His all for us.

1

The Humility of Love

We live in a proud and egotistical generation. It is now consi-dered acceptable and even normal for people to promote them-selves, to praise themselves, and to put themselves first. Pride is seen as a virtue by many. Humility, on the other hand, is viewed as a weakness. Everyone, it seems, is screaming for his own rights and seeking to be recognized as someone important.

The preoccupation with self-esteem, self-love, and self-glory is destroying the foundations upon which our society is built. No cul-ture can survive pride run rampant, for all of society depends on relationships. When people are committed first of all to themselves, relationships disintegrate. And that is just what is happening today, as friendships, marriages, and families fall apart.

Sadly, the preoccupation with self has found its way into the church. Perhaps the fastest-growing phenomenon in modern Christianity is the emphasis on pride, self-esteem, self-image, self-fulfillment, and other manifestations of selfism. Out of it is emerg-ing a new religion of self-centeredness, pride — even arrogance. Voices from every part of the theological spectrum call us to join the self-esteem cult.

Scripture is clear, however, that selfism has no place in Christian theology. Jesus repeatedly taught against pride. In His life and in His teaching He constantly exalted the virtue of humility. Nowhere is that more clear than in John 13.

"HE LOVED THEM TO THE END"

Chapter 13 marks a turning point in John's gospel and the ministry of Jesus Christ. Jesus' public ministry to the nation of Israel has run its course and will soon end in the nation's complete and final rejection of Him as Messiah. On the first day of the week, Jesus had entered Jerusalem in triumph to the enthusiastic shouts of the people. The people nevertheless misunderstood His ministry and His message. The Passover season had arrived, and by Friday He would be utterly rejected and executed. God, however, would turn that execution into the great and final sacrifice for sin, and Jesus would die as the true Passover Lamb.

He had come unto His own people, the Jews, but "His own did not receive Him" (John 1:11). So He had turned away from His public ministry to the intimate fellowship of His disciples.

Now it was the day before Jesus' death, but rather than being preoccupied with thoughts of His death, sin-bearing, and glorification, He was totally consumed with His love for the disciples. Knowing that He was soon to go to the cross to die for the sins of the world, He was still concerned with the needs of twelve men. His love is never impersonal — that is the mystery of it.

In what were literally the last hours before His death, Jesus kept showing His disciples His love over and over. John relates this graphic demonstration:

> Now before the Feast of the Passover, Jesus knowing that His hour had come that He should depart out of this world to the Father, having loved His own who were in the world, He loved them to the end.
>
> And during supper, the devil having already put into the heart of Judas Iscariot, the son of Simon, to betray Him, Jesus, knowing that the Father had given all things into His hands, and that He had come forth from God, and was going back to God, rose from supper, and laid aside His garments; and taking a towel, He girded Himself about. Then He poured water into the basin, and began to wash the disciples' feet, and to wipe them with the towel with which He was girded.
>
> And so He came to Simon Peter. He said to Him, "Lord, do You wash my feet?"
>
> Jesus answered and said to him, "What I do you do not realize now, but you shall understand hereafter."
>
> Peter said to Him, "Never shall You wash my feet!"
>
> Jesus answered Him, "If I do not wash you, you have no part with Me."

Simon Peter said to Him, "Lord, not my feet only but also my hands and my head."

Jesus said to him, "He who has bathed needs only to wash his feet, but is completely clean; and you are clean, but not all of you." For He knew the one who was betraying Him; for this reason He said, "Not all of you are clean."

And so when He had washed their feet, and taken His garments, and reclined at the table again, He said to them, "Do you know what I have done to you? You call Me Teacher and Lord; and you are right, for so I am. If I then, the Lord and the Teacher, washed your feet, you also ought to wash one another's feet. For I gave you an example that you also should do as I did to you. Truly, truly, I say to you, a slave is not greater than his master; neither is one who is sent greater than the one who sent him. If you know these things, you are blessed if you do them."

(John 13:1-17)

It is very likely that Jesus and the disciples had been hiding at Bethany during the final week before the crucifixion. Having come from there (or from anywhere near Jerusalem), they would have had to travel on extremely dirty roads. Naturally, by the time they arrived, their feet were covered with dust from the road.

Everyone in that culture faced the same problem. Sandals did little to keep dirt off the feet, and the roads were either a thick layer of dust or deep masses of mud. At the entrance to every Jewish home was a large pot of water to wash dirty feet. Normally, footwashing was the duty of the lowliest slave. When guests came, that slave had to go to the door and wash their feet — not a pleasant task. In fact, washing feet was probably his most abject duty, and *only* slaves performed it for others. Even the disciples of rabbis were not to wash the feet of their masters — that was uniquely the task of a slave.

As Jesus and His disciples arrived at the upper room, they found no servant to wash their feet. Only days before, Jesus had said to the twelve, "Whoever wishes to be great among you shall be your servant, and whoever wishes to be first among you shall be your slave" (Matthew 20:26-27). If they had given mind and heart to His teaching, one of the twelve would have washed the others' feet, or they would have mutually shared the task. It could have been a beautiful thing, but it never occured to them because of their selfishness. A parallel passage in Luke 22 gives us an idea just how selfish they were and what they were thinking about that evening:

> And there arose also a dispute among them as to which one of them was regarded to be greatest. And He said to them, "The kings of the Gentiles lord it over them; and those who have authority over them are called 'Benefactors.' But not so with you, but let him who is the greatest among you become as the youngest, and the leader as the servant."
>
> (vv. 24-26)

What a sickening picture this is! They were bickering about who was the greatest. And in an argument about who is the greatest, no one is going to get down on the ground and wash feet. The basin was there, the towel was there, and everything was ready. But no one moved to wash the others' feet.

If anyone in that room should have been thinking about the glory that would be his in the kingdom, it was Jesus. Verse 1 says that Jesus knew His hour was come. He was on a divine time schedule, and He knew that He was going to be with the Father. He was conscious also that soon He would be glorified: "Jesus [knew] that the Father had given all things into His hands, and that he had come forth from God, and was going back to God" (v. 3). But instead of being concerned with His glory, and in spite of their selfishness, He focused His attention on clearly revealing His personal love to the twelve that they might be secure in it.

Verse 1 says, "Having loved His own who were in the world, He loved them to the end." "To the end" in the Greek is *eis telos,* and it means this: He loved them to perfection. He loved them to the uttermost. He loved them with total fullness of love. That is the nature of Christ's love, and He showed it repeatedly — even in His death. When He was arrested, He arranged that the disciples would not be arrested. While He was on the cross, He made sure that John would give Mary a home and care for her in years to come. He reached out to a dying thief and saved him. It is amazing that in those last hours of carrying the sins of the world, in the midst of all the pain and suffering He was bearing, He was conscious of that one would-be disciple hanging next to Him. He loves utterly, absolutely, perfectly, totally, completely, unreservedly. At the moment when most men would have been wholly concerned with self, He selflessly humbled Himself to meet the needs of others. Genuine love is like that.

And here is the great lesson of this whole account: Only absolute humility can generate absolute love. It is the nature of love to be selfless, giving. In 1 Corinthians 13:5, Paul says that love "does not seek its own." In fact, to distill the truth of 1 Corinthians 13 into a single statement, we might say that the greatest virtue of love is its humility, for it is the humility of love that proves it and makes it visible.

Christ's love and His humility are inseparable. He could not have been so consumed with a passion for serving others if He had been primarily concerned with Himself.

"LOVE . . . IN DEED AND TRUTH"

How could anyone reject that kind of love? Men do it all the time. Judas did. "And during supper the devil [had] already put into the heart of Judas Iscariot, the son of Simon, to betray Him" (v. 2). Do you see the tragedy of Judas? He was constantly basking in the light, yet living in darkness; experiencing the love of Christ, yet hating Him at the same time.

The contrast between Jesus and Judas is striking. And perhaps that is the reason the Holy Spirit included verse 2 in this passage. Set against the backdrop of Judas's hatred, Jesus' love shines even brighter. We can better understand its magnitude when we understand that in the heart of Judas was the blackest kind of hatred and rejection. The words of love by which Jesus gradually drew the hearts of the other disciples to Himself only pushed Judas further and further away. The teaching by which He uplifted the souls of the other disciples just seemed to drive a stake into the heart of Judas. And everything that Jesus said of love must have been like chafing shackles to Judas. From his fettered greed and his disappointed ambition began to spring jealousy, spite, and hatred — and now he was ready to destroy Christ, if need be.

But the more men hated Jesus and desired to hurt Him, the more it seemed He manifested love to them. It would be easy to understand resentment. It would be easy to understand bitterness. But all Jesus had was love — He even met the greatest injury with supreme love. In a little while He would be kneeling at the feet of Judas, washing them.

Jesus waited until everyone was seated and supper was served. Then, in a devastating act of humility that must have stunned the disciples,

> [Jesus] rose from supper, and laid aside His garments; and taking a towel, He girded Himself about. Then He poured water into the basin, and began to wash the disciples' feet, and to wipe them with the towel with which He was girded.
>
> (vv. 4-5)

With calmness and majesty, in total silence, Jesus stood up, walked over and took the pitcher, and poured the water into the basin. He then removed His outer robe, His belt, and very likely His inner tunic — leaving Him clothed like a slave — put a towel around His waist, and knelt to wash the feet of His disciples, one by one.

Can you imagine how that must have stung the disciples' hearts? Do you feel the pain, the regret, and the sorrow that must have shot through them? One of them could have had the joy of kneeling and washing the feet of Jesus. I am sure they were dumbfounded and brokenhearted. What a painful and profound lesson this was for them!

We, too, can learn from this incident. Sadly, the church is full of people who are standing on their dignity when they ought to be kneeling at the feet of their brothers. The desire for prominence is death to love, death to humility, and death to service. One who is proud and self-centered has no capacity for love or humility. Consequently, any service he may think he is performing for the Lord is a waste.

When you are tempted to think of your dignity, your prestige, or your rights, open your Bible to John 13 and get a good look at Jesus — clothed like a slave, kneeling, washing dirt off the feet of sinful men who are utterly indifferent to His impending death. To go from being God in glory (v. 3) to washing the feet of sinful, inglorious disciples (vv. 3-5) is a long step. Think about this: The majestic, glorious God of the universe comes to earth — that is humility. Then He kneels on the ground to wash the feet of sinful men — that is *indescribable* humility.

You see, for a fisherman to wash the feet of another fisherman is a relatively small sacrifice of dignity. But that Jesus Christ, in whose heart beat the pulse of eternal deity, would stoop and wash the feet of lowly men, that is the greatest kind of humiliation. And that is the nature of genuine humility, as well as the proof of genuine love.

Love has to be more than words. The apostle John wrote, "Let us not love with word or with tongue, but in deed and truth" (1 John 3:18). Love that is real is love expressed in activity, not just words.

"If I Do Not Wash You, You Have No Part with Me"

Here we have one of the most interesting insights into Peter that we see anywhere in Scripture. As Jesus moved from disciple to disciple, He finally arrived at Peter, who must have been completely broken. Peter said with a mixture of remorse and incredulity,

"Lord, do You wash my feet?" (v. 6), and perhaps he pulled back his feet.

Jesus replied to Peter, "What I do you do not realize now, but you shall understand hereafter" (v. 7). Peter was still thinking of the kingdom and of Jesus as King. How could he allow the King to wash his feet? Not until after Jesus' death, resurrection, and ascension would Peter understand the total humiliation of Jesus.

Peter became bolder. He exclaimed, "Never shall You wash my feet!" (v. 8). To emphasize his words, Peter used the strongest form of negation in the Greek language. He called Jesus Lord but acted as if *he* were. This was not praiseworthy modesty on Peter's part.

> Jesus answered him, "If I do not wash you, you have no part with Me."
> Simon Peter said to Him, "Lord, not my feet only, but also my hands and my head."
>
> (vv. 8-9)

That was typical of Peter — he went from one extreme ("Never shall You wash my feet!") to the other ("Not my feet only, but also my hands and my head").

There was profound meaning in Jesus' words "If I do not wash you, you have no part with Me." You see, the typical Jewish mindset could not accept the Messiah humiliated. In Peter's mind, there was no place for Christ to be humiliated like this. Peter had to be made to realize that Christ came to be humiliated. If Peter could not accept this act of humiliation, he would certainly have trouble accepting what Jesus would do for him on the cross.

There is yet another, more profound, truth in Jesus' words. He was moving from the physical illustration of washing feet to the spiritual truth of washing the inner man. Throughout John's gospel, when He dealt with people, Jesus spoke of spiritual truth in physical terms. He had done it when He spoke to Nicodemus, when He spoke to the woman at the well, and when He spoke to the Pharisees. Now He did it with Peter.

Jesus was saying, "Peter, unless you allow Me to wash you in a spiritual way, you are not clean and you have no part with Me." All cleansing in the spiritual realm comes from Christ, and the only way anyone can be clean is if he is washed by regeneration through Jesus Christ (Titus 3:5). No man has a relationship with Jesus Christ unless Christ has cleansed his sins. And no one can enter into the presence of the Lord unless he first submits to that cleansing.

Peter was to learn that truth — he preached it himself in Acts

4:12: "And there is salvation in no one else; for there is no other name under heaven that has been given among men, by which we must be saved." When a man puts his faith in Jesus Christ, he is clean, and not until then.

"HE WHO HAS BATHED . . . IS COMPLETELY CLEAN"

Thinking that the Lord was speaking of physical cleansing, Peter offered his hands and head — everything. He still did not see the full spiritual meaning but said in essence, "Whatever washing you have got to offer me that makes me a part of You, I want it."

Jesus, still speaking of spiritual washing, said, "He who has bathed needs only to wash his feet, but is completely clean; and you are clean" (v. 10). There is a difference between a bath and a footwashing. In the culture of that day, a man took a bath in the morning to get himself completely clean. As he went through the day, he washed his feet from time to time, because of the dusty roads, but he did not keep on taking baths. All he needed was to wash the dirt off his feet when he entered someone's home.

Jesus was saying this: Once your inner man has been bathed in redemption, you are clean. From that point on, you do not need a new bath — you do not need to be redeemed again — every time you commit a sin. All God has to do is daily get the dust off your feet. Positionally, you are clean (as He told Peter in verse 10), but on the practical side, you need washing every day, as you walk through the world and get dirty feet.

That spiritual washing of the feet is what 1 John 1:9 refers to: "If we confess our sins, He is faithful and righteous to forgive us our sins and to cleanse us [literally, 'keep on cleansing us'] from all unrighteousness."

Jesus knew which of the disciples were truly cleansed by redemption. Furthermore, He knew what Judas's plans for the evening were: "For He knew the one who was betraying Him; for this reason He said, 'Not all of you are clean' " (vv. 11). That should have pricked the heart of Judas.

Judas knew what He meant. Those words, combined with Jesus' washing his feet, were the last loving appeal for Judas not to do what he was planning to do. What was going through the mind of Judas as Jesus knelt washing his feet? Whatever it was, it had no deterring effect on Judas.

"YOU ALSO OUGHT TO WASH ONE ANOTHER'S FEET"

Notice what happened when Jesus finished washing their feet:

> When He had washed their feet, and taken His garments, and re-
> clined at the table again, He said to them, "Do you know what I
> have done to you? You call Me Teacher and Lord; and you are
> right, for so I am. If I then, the Lord and the Teacher, washed
> your feet, you also ought to wash one another's feet. For I gave
> you an example that you also should do as I did to you. Truly, tru-
> ly, I say to you, a slave is not greater than his master; neither is
> one who is sent greater than the one who sent him. If you know
> these things, you are blessed if you do them."
>
> (vv. 12-17)

Having inserted a parenthetical lesson on salvation — a sort of
theological interlude — Jesus returned to the real point He was
teaching His disciples: They needed to begin to operate on the basis of humility.

He argued from the greater to the lesser. If the Lord of glory was
willing to gird Himself with a towel, take upon Himself the form of
a servant, act like a slave, and wash the dirty feet of sinful disciples,
it was reasonable that the disciples should be willing to wash each
other's feet.

Many people believe that in John 13 Jesus was instituting an or-
dinance for the church. Some churches practice footwashing in a
ritual similar to the way we have baptism and Communion. I have
no quarrel with that, but I do not believe that is what is being taught
in this passage. Jesus was not advocating a formal, ritualistic
footwashing service.

Verse 15 says, "I gave you an example that you also should do as
I did to you." The word *as* is a translation of the Greek word *kathos*,
which means "according as." If Jesus were establishing footwashing
as a pattern of ritual to be practiced in the church, He would have
used the Greek word *ho*, which means "that which." Then He
would have been saying, "I have given you an example that you
should do *what* I have done to you."

But He was not saying, "Do the same thing I have done." He was
saying, "Behave in the same manner as I have behaved." The example we are to follow is not the washing of feet; it is His humility.
Do not minimize the lesson by making footwashing the important
point of John 13. Jesus' humility was the real lesson — and it was a
practical humility that should govern every area of life, every day of
life, in every experience of life.

The result of that kind of humility is always loving service — doing the menial and humiliating tasks for the glory of Jesus Christ.
That demolishes most of the popular ideas of what constitutes spiri-

tuality. Some people seem to think that the nearer you get to God the further you must be from men, but that is not true. Actual proximity to God is to serve someone else.

In terms of sacrificing to serve others, there was never anything Jesus was unwilling to do. Why should we be different? We are not greater than the Lord: "Truly, truly, I say to you, a slave is not greater than his master; neither is one who is sent greater than the one who sent him. If you know these things, you are blessed [happy] if you do them" (vv. 16-17).

Do you want to be blessedly fulfilled and happy? Develop a servant's heart. We are His bondservants, and a servant is not greater than his master. If Jesus can step down from a position of deity to become a man, and then further humble Himself to be a servant and wash the feet of twelve undeserving sinners, we ought to be willing to suffer any indignity to serve Him. That is true love and true humility.

2
Unmasking the Betrayer

Judas Iscariot, who betrayed the Son of God with a kiss, has become the most detested person in the annals of human history. His personality is the darkest in the chronicle of the world, and the name *Judas* itself bears a stigma, reflecting the scorn for him that burns within us. The New Testament writers disdain Judas to such a degree that in every list of the disciples given in the gospels Judas is listed last, with a note of contempt after his name.

Hatred for Judas was so deep in the years following the closing of the New Testament that several incredible legends about him evolved. They described bizarre occurrences, characterizing Judas as ugly, evil, and totally repugnant. One, recorded in the apocryphal Coptic Narrative, said that Judas, having betrayed Christ, was infested with maggots. Consequently, his body became so bloated that on one occasion, when he was trying to drive a cart through a gate, his body hit the gate and exploded, and maggots blew all over the wall. Obviously, that story is not true, but it shows the high level of contempt for Judas in the early centuries.

When I was in seminary, I wrote my dissertation on the subject of Judas. During the year that I spent working on it, and since then, I have found it extremely difficult to write or speak on the subject of Judas. Sin is never more grotesque than it is in the life of Judas. When we study Judas and his motivations, we are prying close to the activity of Satan. But there are good reasons for examining Judas and his sin. For one thing, to understand Jesus' love in its fullness, it helps to look at the life of Judas, because despite the awfulness of Judas's sin, Jesus reached out to him in love.

Jesus and Judas

In John 13:17-30, Jesus and Judas come head to head. We see clearly at this point the evil of Judas contrasted with the absolute purity of Jesus Christ. The diabolical deed that had been festering in the heart of Judas — the treachery he had already begun to perpetrate — was pushed to its climax, and Judas was unmasked as the betrayer.

Jesus speaks at the beginning of this powerful passage:

> "If you know these things, you are blessed if you do them. I do not speak of all of you. I know the ones I have chosen; but it is that the Scripture may be fulfilled, 'He who eats My bread has lifted up his heel against Me.' From now on I am telling you before it comes to pass, so that when it does occur, you may believe that I am He. Truly, truly, I say to you, he who receives whomever I send receives Me; and he who receives Me receives Him who sent Me."
>
> When Jesus had said this, He became troubled in spirit, and testified, and said, "Truly, truly, I say to you, that one of you will betray Me."
>
> The disciples began looking at one another, at a loss to know of which one He was speaking. There was reclining on Jesus' breast one of His disciples, whom Jesus loved. Simon Peter therefore gestured to him, and said to him, "Tell us who it is of whom He is speaking."
>
> He, leaning back thus on Jesus' breast, said to Him, "Lord, who is it?"
>
> Jesus therefore answered, "That is the one for whom I shall dip the morsel and give it to him." So when He had dipped the morsel, He took and gave it to Judas, the son of Simon Iscariot.
>
> And after the morsel, Satan then entered into him. Jesus therefore said to him, "What you do, do quickly."
>
> Now no one of those reclining at the table knew for what purpose He had said this to him. For some were suppposing, because Judas had the money box, that Jesus was saying to him, "Buy the things we have need of for the feast"; or else, that he should give something to the poor.
>
> And so after receiving the morsel he went out immediately; and it was night.

There we see Jesus and Judas — the epitome of opposites: the perfect One and the absolutely wretched; the best and the worst. The purity of Jesus and the vileness of Judas are emphasized by the contrast.

Judas was an ultimate tragedy — probably the greatest tragedy that ever lived. He was the perfect and prime example of what it means to have opportunity and then lose it. What he became is all the more terrible because of the glorious beginning he had. Judas followed the same Christ as the others. For three years, day in and day out, he occupied himself with Jesus Christ. He saw the same miracles, heard the same words, performed some of the same ministries, was esteemed in the same way the other disciples were esteemed — yet he did not become what the others became. In fact, he became the very opposite. While they were growing into true apostles and saints of God, he was progressively turning into a vile, calculating tool of Satan.

For three years, he moved and walked with Jesus. Initially, he must have shared the same hope of the kingdom that the other disciples had. He likely believed that Jesus was the Messiah. He, too, had left all and followed Jesus. Certainly along the line he became greedy, but it is doubtful that he joined the apostles for what money he could get, because they never really had any. Perhaps his motive at the outset was just to get in on the kingdom that Jesus would bring.

Whatever his character at the beginning, he gradually became the treacherous man who betrayed Christ, a man who had no thought for anyone but himself, a man who finally wanted only to get as much money as he could and get out.

Greed, ambition, and worldliness had crept into his heart, and avarice had become his besetting sin. Perhaps he was disappointed because of unfulfilled expectations of an earthly kingdom. Maybe he was tormented by the unbearable rebuke of the presence of Christ. Surely it created a great tension in his heart to be constantly in the presence of sinless purity and yet be so infested with vileness. Perhaps, too, he began to sense that the eye of the Master could see who he was and what he was. Or it may be that all those things had begun to eat at him.

Whatever the reasons, he ended in absolute disaster, the greatest example of lost opportunity the world has ever seen. On the night he betrayed Jesus, he was so prepared to do Satan's bidding that Satan was able to enter him and take complete control of him. A few days before that in Bethany, he had met with the leaders of Israel and bargained for thirty pieces of silver, the price of a slave — some twenty to twenty-five dollars. Now his evil deed came to full fruition on the eve of the crucifixion.

Jesus and his disciples (including Judas) were in the upper room. The vile traitor was sitting there, having already made his bargain to betray Jesus for thirty pieces of silver. He had already carried out the initiation of it, and now he had returned to spend these moments with the disciples, looking for the right moment to betray Jesus' presence to the Jewish leaders.

Jesus had revealed in verse 10 that He knew Judas's heart, saying, " 'You are clean, but not all of you.' For He knew the one who was betraying Him" (vv. 10-11). Judas had been sitting there all through Jesus' wonderful lesson on humility and His washing of the disciples' feet. Jesus had even washed his feet. Judas sat there, the wretched hypocrite, letting the blessed Lord wash his feet, while in his head he was plotting the betrayal of Jesus, hardly able to wait until he could get his hands on the thirty coins.

Even though Jesus knew what Judas was about to do, He washed his feet. It was only one example of the marvelous love of Jesus Christ and the way He reached out to Judas. The measures He took to win Judas even at that late hour made His love all the more wonderful. One would think the experience of having Jesus wash his feet would have been enough to break any man's heart. But not Judas's, so cold was he. He was determined to sell the Master to the executioners.

THE BLESSED AND THE CURSED

Having taught by example a wonderful lesson on humility, Jesus then carefully explained its meaning. He concluded His discourse by saying, "If you know these things, you are blessed if you do them" (v. 17). *Blessed,* of course, is a synonym for *happy.* One who learns how to show humble love, who is willing to bow down to the ground and serve another believer, is rewarded with true happiness. When you condescend in that kind of love, when you are willing to do a menial duty for the sake of another, when you do not care about exalting yourself to predominance in every situation — when you humble yourself — you will be happy.

But Jesus could not speak of blessedness without speaking of the contrast and what it was to be cursed. He did not think of happiness without thinking of tragedy and unhappiness. Although the breath of happiness was coming from His lips, at the same time His mind began to fill with thoughts of the cursed Judas sitting beside Him. And so, He turns in verse 18 from the happy disciples to the cursed one, Judas. From verses 18 to 30 the dialogue focuses on Judas himself. This is the final confrontation between Jesus and Judas, leaving only a kiss later on.

It is important to understand why Jesus brought up the subject of His betrayal at this point. Unless Jesus had in some way prepared the disciples for what was about to happen, it could have had a serious, adverse effect on them. If Judas had suddenly and without warning betrayed Jesus, the disciples might have concluded that Jesus was not all He claimed to be; otherwise He would have known what Judas was like and would never have chosen him. So Jesus said, "I know the ones I have chosen; but it is that the Scripture may be fulfilled, 'He who eats My bread has lifted up his heel against Me.' From now on I am telling you before it comes to pass, so that when it does occur, you may believe that I am He" (v. 18).

It would be easy to pass by this statement and miss the point. Jesus wanted to be sure that they did not think He was surprised by what Judas was about to do. He therefore said in effect to those disciples, "I know I chose Judas. I did it, not by accident, not in ignorance, but in order that Scripture might be fulfilled." He chose Judas because Judas was necessary to bring about His death, which was itself necessary to bring about the redemption of the world.

Prophecy was clear that Christ would be betrayed by a close friend. Why did Jesus choose Judas, then? He chose him to fulfill prophecy — not only the prophecy specifically about Judas but also the prophecies of His own death. Somebody had to bring it to pass, and Judas was more than willing. God used the wrath of Judas to praise Him, and through the deed that Judas did He brought salvation. Judas meant it for evil, but God used it for good (cf. Genesis 50:20).

GOD'S PLAN AND JUDAS'S PLOT

You see, Judas fit right into the divine master plan. Judas's betrayal was predicted in detail in the Old Testament. Psalm 41:9 says,

> Even my close friend, in whom I trusted,
> Who ate my bread,
> Has lifted up his heel against me.

Psalm 41 had historical, as well as prophetic, meaning. It was David's lament over his own betrayal by his trusted adviser Ahithophel. David had a wayward son named Absalom. Absalom decided to start a rebellion, overthrow his father, and take over the throne. Ahithophel turned against David and joined Absalom's rebellion. The picture of David and Ahithophel in Psalm 41 is fulfilled in a greater sense in Jesus and Judas. The phrase "lifted up his heel" portrays brutal violence, the lifting up of a heel and the driving of that heel into the neck of the victim. That is the picture of Judas.

Having wounded his enemy, who now lies on the ground, he takes the giant heel and crushes his neck.

Psalm 55 contains another clear prophecy of Judas and his betrayal. Imagine Jesus speaking these words:

> For it is not an enemy who reproaches me,
> Then I could bear it;
> Nor is it one who hates me who has exalted himself against me.
> Then I could hide myself from him.
> But it is you, a man my equal,
> My companion and my familiar friend.
> We who had sweet fellowship together,
> Walked in the house of God in the throng. . . .
>
> He has put forth his hands against those who were at peace with
>   him;
> He has violated his covenant.
> His speech was smoother than butter,
> But his heart was war;
> His words were softer than oil,
> Yet they were drawn swords.
>
> (vv. 12-14; 20-21)

Zechariah contains a prophecy about the betrayal of Christ by Judas in even more detail. The book gives the exact price Judas was paid for his treachery, just as it is recorded in the New Testament. Zechariah 11:12-13 prophetically gives the words Judas spoke to the Jewish leaders:

> And I said to them, "If it is good in your sight, give me my wages; but if not, never mind!" So they weighed out thirty shekels of silver as my wages. Then the Lord said to me, "Throw it to the potter, that magnificent price at which I was valued by them." So I took the thirty shekels of silver and threw them to the potter in the house of the Lord.

That describes to the letter what Judas did after the death of Jesus Christ. He took the thirty shekels back to the house of the Lord and threw them down. Matthew 27 says that the thirty coins were picked up and used to buy a potter's field, exactly fulfilling the prophecy of Zechariah 11.

DIVINE SOVEREIGNTY AND HUMAN CHOICE

Jesus' choosing of Judas was no accident. Long before Judas was born, his hatred of Jesus Christ was planned by divine design — predestined in the plan of God from eternity past. In John 17:12, Jesus, praying to the Father, says of the disciples, "While I was with them, I was keeping them in Thy name which Thou hast given Me; and I guarded them, and no one of them perished but the son of perdition, that the Scripture might be fulfilled."

Understand, Judas's role was not apart from his own will. Even though God ordained that Judas would be the one who would betray Christ, it was not apart from the desire of Judas. Judas was no robot. Our Lord did not simply allocate to an unwilling Judas the role of the villain in the crucifixion. Such a thing would have been inconsistent with the character of Jesus Christ, and it would have been inconsistent with the historical record. Throughout the ministry of Jesus, He endeavored to drive Judas to repentance, time and time again, with His love, His pleas, and His rebukes. So although Judas's treachery fit into the plan of God, God did not design him as a treacherous man. He became a traitor to Christ by his own choice. God merely designed his treachery into the divine plan. He took Judas, wretched as he was, and fitted him into His plan. If God had been responsible for making Judas what he was, Jesus would have pitied him rather than rebuked him.

Judas Iscariot, then, was the chosen instrument of God, not apart from his own will, to betray Christ and bring about His death (John 17:12). This wretched man — evil as he was, by his own desire — was designed into God's plan. And to show that it was not God's will apart from Judas's will, all the way along and at every opportunity, Jesus gave him warnings and pleas to bring him to repentance and salvation. And at every point he turned them down. We see that clearly in John 13.

WALKING WITH JESUS AND FOLLOWING SATAN

Judas, through his life of treachery, supplies sinners with a solemn warning. We learn from the example of Judas that a person can be very near to Jesus Christ and yet be lost and damned forever. Nobody was closer to Christ than the twelve. Judas was one of them, and he is in hell today, because although he may have given intellectual assent to the truth, he never embraced Christ with heartfelt faith.

Judas was not deceived; he was a phony. He understood the truth, and he posed as a believer. Furthermore, he was good at it — the cleverest hypocrite we read about in all the Scriptures, for no one ever suspected him. He had everyone fooled except Jesus, who knew his heart.

And mark it, wherever God's work is done, there are impostors like Judas. There will always be hypocrites among the brethren. The favorite trick of Satan and those he employs is to "disguise themselves as servants of righteousness" (2 Corinthians 11:15). The devil is a master at making his work *look* good — and he is busily at work among the Lord's people.

TRUTH AND CONSEQUENCES

Prior to this time Jesus had maintained secrecy about Judas's hypocrisy. Now He was determined to reveal the truth, knowing that if the other eleven disciples were taken by surprise, their faith might be undermined. He wanted them to know that He Himself was not being taken by surprise, that God is never any man's victim. He wanted to insure that when He was gone the disciples' faith would be strong.

In revealing to them the truth about Judas, He also affirmed His deity irrefutably. In verse 19, Jesus says, "I am telling you before it comes to pass, so that when it does occur, you may believe that I am." (The "He" in that verse is not in the original Greek text.)

"I AM" is God's name (Exodus 3:14). Jesus was saying, "I want you to know that I am God, and I knew this would happen," thereby affirming His name and establishing His omniscience. Nothing is hidden from His sight. He knows what goes on in Christians' hearts, but more than that, He knows what goes on in the hearts of unregenerate people as well. In John 5:42, Jesus, talking to unbelieving Jews, says, "But I know you, that you do not have the love of God in yourselves." He knows the heart of every man, believer or unbeliever. He reads it like an open book.

THE APOSTLES AND THE BETRAYER

In verse 20, after affirming His deity, Jesus, still speaking of His imminent betrayal, says, "Truly, truly, I say to you, he who receives whomever I send receives Me; and he who receives Me receives Him who sent Me." Initially, that statement does not seem to fit the context of what Jesus is saying in the passage as a whole. But a close look reveals that it fits beautifully.

We do not know what went on in the gap between verses 19 and 20. But you can imagine that when the disciples found out about the betrayal, they might have assumed that because of the failure of one of them, credibility was destroyed for the rest. They might have assumed that a traitor among the disciples would lower the standing of them all. If Jesus went to the cross, they must have thought, the messianic hope would be gone. Their ministry would be over. They might as well forget about the kingdom. And, remember, Jesus had just been stressing the importance of humility. Perhaps they were beginning to think that He was telling them to forget about their high calling.

So what Jesus was saying was this: "No matter what happens, it does not lower your commission, and it does not alter your calling. You are still my representatives. Although there is a traitor among you, that does not affect your high calling. The treachery of Judas must never lower your estimate of apostolic responsibility." It was a tremendous lesson. Jesus was saying, "When you go out there and preach, if they receive you they are receiving Me. And if they receive Me, they are receiving the Father who sent Me. Your commission is that high. You represent God in the world."

When Christ was crucified, and Judas turned out to be a rotten hypocrite, and the whole world seemed to be collapsing, it was easy for the disciples to hit bottom spiritually and emotionally. Therefore, Jesus took the opportunity to elevate the eleven and to encourage them to keep their eyes on their calling and on their ministry, where they belonged.

We need to be aware of that truth as well. No matter what Satanic opposition we run into, no matter how frustrating the work becomes, nothing can lower our commission. I recently talked to a discouraged man who is in the Lord's service. He was facing so much opposition he was beginning to wonder if he was in the right work.

Opposition is to be expected, I told him. Anything we do for God is going to meet with opposition. If every missionary looked at a mission field and said, "Oh, they might not believe me over there," we would never get anything done. Just because it is going to be difficult, and just because there is going to be opposition, your calling is not lowered. We are Christ's ambassadors in the world. Those who reject us reject Christ, so regardless of what happens, we stand with Him. That is as high as you can get.

When a believer moves out into the world, he represents Jesus Christ. Paul says in 2 Corinthians 5:20, "Therefore, we are ambassadors for Christ, as though God were entreating through us; we beg you on behalf of Christ, be reconciled to God." In Galatians 4:14, the apostle Paul says, "You received me as an angel of God, as Christ Jesus Himself." And that is the way everybody ought to receive a believer. When a man rejects our witness for Christ, he rejects Jesus and he rejects God. That is how strategically important believers are. Notice that in verse 20 Jesus uses the word "whomever." That refers to ambassadors of Jesus Christ in every age, including those of us who represent Him today.

Have you ever heard someone use hypocrites as an excuse for not following Christ? People often say, "There are too many hypocrites in the church for me." Or, "Well, we don't go to church, because we went back when I was nine and we saw a hypocrite. Haven't been back in forty-two years!" That will be a pathetic excuse when they rattle it off to God in the day of judgment.

But it is true that there are too many hypocrites in the church. They are everywhere. And one hypocrite is one too many. But the fact that some are hypocrites does not diminish the glory of God or lower the high calling of every true child of God. One betrayer among the apostles did not tarnish the commission of the rest.

WHEAT AND TARES

In Matthew 13:24-30, Jesus gives this parable:

> The kingdom of heaven may be compared to a man who sowed good seed in his field. But while men were sleeping, his enemy came and sowed tares also among the wheat, and went away. But when the wheat sprang up and bore grain, then the tares became evident also.
>
> And the slaves of the landowner came and said to him, "Sir, did you not sow good seed in your field? How then does it have tares?"
>
> And he said to them, "An enemy has done this!" And the slaves said to him, "Do you want us, then, to go and gather them up?" But he said, "No; lest while you are gathering up the tares, you may root up the wheat with them. Allow both to grow together until the harvest; and in the time of harvest I will say to the reapers, 'First gather up the tares and bind them in bundles to burn them up; but gather the wheat into my barn.' "

In other words, it is hard to tell the difference between wheat and tares before they are ready for harvest. And though there may be some telltale signs, we cannot always tell the difference between the true people of God and the hypocrites. If we knew which was which, we could go to every hypocrite individually and warn him of the danger of his hypocrisy. But we cannot read people's hearts. Yet someday Jesus is going to reveal who is true and who is false, and He will divide accordingly.

THE TROUBLED HEART AND THE HARDENED HEART

Unmasking Judas's betrayal must have caused deep anguish

within the heart of Jesus. "When Jesus had said this, He became troubled in spirit, and testified, and said, 'Truly, truly, I say to you, that one of you will betray Me' " (v. 21). What troubled Him? Possibly a number of things: He was troubled because of His unrequited love for Judas; He was troubled because of the ingratitude in Judas's heart; He was troubled because he had a deep hatred of sin, and yet sitting at the same table with Him was sin incarnate; He was troubled because of the hypocrisy of the one about to betray Him; He was troubled because He knew Judas faced an eternal destiny in hell; He was troubled because with His omnipotence He could see Satan moving around Judas; He was troubled because He sensed all that sin and death meant. But perhaps most of all He was troubled because He had an awareness that Judas was a classic illustration of the wretchedness of sin, which He would have to bear in His own body on the next day.

In His anguish, He said, "One of you will betray Me." Imagine the shock that must have rattled through the disciples. Their hearts must have raced. One of those at the table, one of those whose feet Jesus had just washed, one of their own, close group was about to betray the Master. One of them was plotting to use his intimacy with Christ to guide the enemy to Him so that they might kill Him. It must have been difficult for them to fathom that one of their own group could have such treachery in his heart.

In fact, the disciples could not imagine whom He was talking about. John says they "began looking at one another, at a loss to know of which one He was speaking" (v. 22). Matthew says they all said, "Is it I? Is it I?" And Judas, the hypocrite, even said, "Surely it is not I, Rabbi?" (Matthew 26:25).

LOVE AND TREACHERY

It is noteworthy that the disciples were so perplexed. It proves that Jesus had shown love to Judas for three years, even though He knew Judas would betray Him in the end. If Jesus had ever treated Judas any differently from the way He treated the other disciples — if He had been more distant or had shown resentment — they would have known immediately that Judas was the betrayer. If Jesus had harbored any bitterness for what He knew Judas would ultimately do, it would have come out in the way He talked to him. But, evidently, for three years He had been gentle, loving, and kind to Judas, treating Him in exactly the same manner He treated the other eleven. They thought of him as one of the group, and no one suspected him.

In fact, they must have had a great deal of trust in him. Judas was treasurer of the group. And hardhearted Judas had just played his game, all the way along. He had the behavior of a saint but the heart of a sinner. He must have come to hate Christ deeply.

The hatred of Judas and the love of John make an interesting contrast. Picture the scene around the table. The table itself was U-shaped. In accordance with the customs of the time, the disciples were not seated on chairs but rather were reclining on couches. The table was a low, solid block with the couches around it. Jesus was at the center, at the deepest part of the table. On each side of Him were the guests of honor. The other guests were positioned at the remaining places around the table. All at the table lay on their left sides, resting on their left elbows and using their right hands to eat. Thus the one who was on the right of Jesus had his head close to His heart. From a distance, it looked as though he were reclining on the breast of Jesus.

John, who wrote this account, often referred to himself as "the disciple whom Jesus loved" (21:20; cf. 21:24). It was not that Jesus loved him more than He loved the others, but rather that John was completely overwhelmed with the concept that Jesus loved him at all. Moreover, John was consumed with love for the Lord. He loved Jesus as much as Judas hated him.

John was reclining next to Jesus: "There was reclining on Jesus' breast one of His disciples, whom Jesus loved. Simon Peter therefore gestured to him, and said to him, 'Tell us who it is of whom He is speaking' " (vv. 23-24). Peter silently motioned to John to ask Jesus who the betrayer would be. So John leaned up and whispered, "Lord, who is it?" When he turned to speak with Him, Christ would be very close.

"Jesus therefore answered, 'That is the one for whom I shall dip the morsel and give it to him.' So when He had dipped the morsel, He took and gave it to Judas, the son of Simon Iscariot" (v. 26). Jesus' answer to Peter and John was really a final appeal of love to Judas. "The morsel" was a piece broken from some of the unleavened cakes that would have been on the table as a part of the Passover feast. Also on the table would have been a dish called *cheshireth*, filled with bitter herbs, vinegar, salt, and mashed fruit, consisting of dates, figs, raisins, and water — all mixed together into a pasty substance. They would have eaten it with the unleavened bread like a dip.

It was a mark of honor for the host to dip a morsel into the *cheshireth* and give it to the guest of honor. And Jesus, kindly, in a gesture of love toward Judas, dipped the morsel and gave it to Judas, as if Judas were the guest of honor. One would think that all Jesus had done for Judas that night would have broken his heart, but it did not. Judas was an apostate. His heart was hardened, and nothing Jesus could do for him would break it. Salvation for him was now impossible. He had become the classic example of the kind of person spoken of in Hebrews 6, who has "once been enlightened and [has] tasted of the heavenly gift and [has] been made a [partaker] of the Holy Spirit, and [has] tasted the good word of God and the powers of the age to come, and then [has] fallen away" (Hebrews 6:4-6). Judas had seen and experienced and tasted all those things, but he never had embraced them with true faith.

The writer to the Hebrews says of those like Judas, "It is impossible to renew them again to repentance, since they again crucify to themselves the Son of God, and put Him to open shame" (v. 6).

Judas was so confirmed in his apostasy that literally he became possessed by Satan. Verse 27 of John 13 says, "And after the morsel, Satan then entered into him. Jesus therefore said to him, 'What you do, do quickly.' " Judas had been duped by Satan, had been flirting with Satan. Satan had already put it in his heart to betray Christ, and now Satan moved in and took over. In that awful moment, the evil will of Judas overcame the last and most powerful offer of Jesus Christ's love, and the sin against the Holy Spirit was finalized. In that moment, Judas was damned to hell forever. He had spurned the love of Christ for the last time, and his eternity was sealed.

DAY AND NIGHT

Jesus' attitude toward Judas immediately changed. He was through with him. Judas had crossed the line of grace, and no more could Jesus reach out to him. The difference was immediate, radical — like day and night. Jesus had been reaching out to Judas in love, but Judas was confirmed in his stubborn apostasy. All Jesus wanted now was to get rid of him.

Notice that Satan and Jesus were now giving Judas the same direction. Satan said, "Betray Him." Christ said, "Do it quickly." Judas was clearly determined to betray Christ, Satan was determined to try to destroy Him, and Christ was determined to die for the sins of the world. But Jesus would shatter Satan's plan by exploding out of the grave.

None of the disciples caught the significance of what was occurring. "Now no one of those reclining at the table knew for what purpose He had said this to him. For some were supposing, because Judas had the money box, that Jesus was saying to him, 'Buy the things we have need of for the feast'; or else, that he should give something to the poor" (vv. 28-29). They thought Judas was going shopping or was going out to dispense some charity at the Passover season.

"And so after receiving the morsel he went out immediately; and it was night" (v. 30). There he went, a solitary figure, leaving the room, to enter the eternity of hell. The Bible does not say where he went, but evidently he went to finalize his deal with the Sanhedrin. And when he went out, it was night. For Judas, who had walked with Jesus and yet stayed in darkness, the hours of daylight and opportunity were over. It was more than mere physical night; it was eternal night in the soul of Judas. It is always night when a man goes out of the presence of Jesus Christ.

There are Judases in every age. Perhaps they are more common than ever today. The professing church is full of people who are selling out Jesus Christ, "crucify[ing] to themselves the Son of God, and put[ing] Him to open shame" (Hebrews 6:6). There are many who have eaten at His table and then lifted their heel against Him. And the greatest tragedy still is only their own ultimate disaster. A poem I once read includes these poignant words:

> Still as of old,
> By himself is priced.
> For thirty pieces Judas sold
> Himself, not Christ.

Be sure that you make the most of your opportunities. Be sure that you are not a hypocrite. If we learn anything from the life of Judas it is that the greatest spiritual privileges may be neutralized by illicit passion. A life that is lived in the face of the unclouded sun may yet end in a night of despair.

3

The Marks of the Committed Christian

Historically, Christians have displayed a number of different kinds of symbols to mark their identity as believers. Lapel pins and neck chains with gold crosses are nothing new. They have been used almost since the beginning of Christianity as marks of identification for believers. In recent years, bumper stickers, posters, tee shirts, decorated Bibles, and jackets with embroidered insignia all have been used by people trying to identify themselves as Christians. I do not have any argument with such symbols, except that they are totally superficial — only as deep as the surface to which they are attached.

As a Christian, whether you wear a button, display a bumper sticker, or use any other kind of visible symbol is of no real consequence. (In fact, the way some Christians drive, they would be well advised to take off their bumper stickers.) More important, and infinitely more definitive than all the pins and stickers and buttons, are the internal, spiritual signs of a true believer.

In John 13:31-38, Jesus gives three distinguishing marks of a committed Christian. Having dismissed Judas to leave His presence eternally, Jesus turned to the eleven remaining disciples and gave them a valedictory address, a farewell speech.

> When therefore he had gone out, Jesus said, "Now is the Son of Man glorified, and God is glorified in Him; if God is glorified in Him, God will also glorify Him in Himself and will glorify Him

immediately. Little children, I am with you a little while longer. You shall seek Me; and as I said to the Jews, I now say to you also, 'Where I am going, you cannot come.'

"A new commandment I give to you, that you love one another, even as I have loved you, that you also love one another. By this all men will know that you are My disciples, if you have love for one another."

Simon Peter said to Him, "Lord, where are You going?"

Jesus answered, "Where I go, you cannot follow Me now; but you shall follow later."

Peter said to Him,"Lord, why can I not follow You right now? I will lay down my life for You."

Jesus answered, "Will you lay down your life for Me? Truly, truly, I say to you, a cock shall not crow, until you deny Me three times."

That passage introduces Jesus' last commission to His disciples before He went to the cross. His farewell message, which continues through John 16, contains every ingredient we need to know about discipleship. In fact, the basics of Paul's teaching on the subject of discipleship come right out of this portion of John. Thus these concluding words of our Lord on His last evening with His disciples are strategic to our understanding of what Christ expects of us as believers. Here Jesus gives three distinguishing marks of a committed Christian. These ingredients should be evident in the life of every disciple.

An Unending Preoccupation with the Glory of God

The committed Christian is preoccupied and absorbed with his Lord's glory. The very purpose for which we exist is to give glory to God; therefore, it is right that a preoccupation with the glory of God is the first mark of a committed Christian. He is concerned only with living to give glory to God. He is not concerned about himself. He is not preoccupied with his own glory. He is not worried about what brings honor to him. He is not on a popularity binge. He is not trying to climb the ladder, to get something bigger and better for himself.

His greatest concern is his Lord's glory. He lives in such a manner that whatever he does brings glory to his Lord. He realizes that it does not matter what people think of him, but only that they glorify God. His motive, his theme, his goal, his reason, his purpose is to give the Lord glory in everything he does. His life reflects the attributes of God, and God is praised by the way he lives.

Jesus taught His disciples that perspective both by example and by precept:

> When therefore [Judas] had gone out, Jesus said, "Now is the Son of Man glorified, and God is glorified in Him; if God is glorified in Him, God will also gloify Him in Himself and will glorify Him immediately. Little children, I am with you a little while longer. You shall seek Me; and as I said to the Jews, I now say to you also, 'Where I am going, you cannot come.' "
>
> (vv. 31-33)

Reading that first phrase, we can almost sense a sigh of relief from our Lord. Now that Judas was gone, He could speak freely to His disciples. God incarnate, Jesus Christ, had come to earth in humility. He had restricted the full manifestation of His glory and subjected Himself to human frailty, though He never sinned. For thirty-three years His glory had been shrouded in human flesh. By the next day He would be in His glory again. All the attributes of God would be on display in Him.

With His coming glory in mind, Jesus made three distinct statements. Each was unique and important.

"NOW IS THE SON OF MAN GLORIFIED"

The first is in verse 31, a great statement of anticipation: "Now is the Son of Man glorified." Judas had begun to set everything in motion. Already he had initiated and had been paid for the betrayal, and he was moving about, getting everything set. In just a few hours Jesus and the disciples would go into the Garden of Gethsemane, where Christ would continue His teaching. There Judas would march in with the soldiers, and the events would begin that would lead to Jesus' death. It was right around the corner, and Jesus was ready to die — to be glorified.

Even though the cross looked like shame, disgrace, and disaster, it was glory. At first it may seem difficult to understand how death can be glory, especially death by crucifixion. In His death our Lord experienced the deepest shame, humiliation, infamy, and mockery, and the vilest accusations and insults men could throw at Him. He died hanging between thieves, receiving the agony of sin and separation from God. Yet knowing He was facing all of that, Jesus could say, "Now is the Son of Man glorified."

How was there glory in the cross? There Jesus performed the greatest work in the history of the universe. In His death He brought to pass the salvation of damned sinners, destroyed sin, and defeated Satan. He paid the price of God's justice and purchased for Himself all the elect of God. In dying for sin, He rendered His life a sweet-smelling savor to God, a sacrifice more pure and blessed than any sacrifice ever offered. And when the offended justice of God and the broken law were fully satisfied, Jesus concluded His work by saying, "It is finished." He had accomplished the redemption of the human race, satisfied the justice of God, repaired the broken law, and set men free. In all heaven and earth, no act is so worthy of praise and honor and full glory.

"AND GOD IS GLORIFIED IN HIM"

Jesus made a second statement about glory. Not only was He glorified, but God was also glorified in Him.

God is glorified through the details of the gospel. When Jesus said, "Now is the Son of Man glorified, and God is glorified in Him" (v. 31), He was speaking of His death, burial, resurrection, exaltation, and coming again. All the glory He was speaking of came through those things. And those things are the elements of the gospel message.

One of the greatest ways we can give glory to God is to declare the gospel. The message of the gospel radiates the glory of God like nothing else in all the universe. When we declare the gospel we are declaring the clearest and most powerful aspects of God's glory. Thus, in a sense, witnessing is one of the highest and purest forms of worship, because it most clearly affirms the glory of God.

God's glory is wrapped up in His attributes. His love, mercy, grace, wisdom, omniscience, omnipotence, omnipresence — all the attributes of God — reflect and declare His glory. We glorify God when we in any way praise or acknowledge or experience or display His attributes. When we are examples of His love, for instance, we glorify Him. When we acknowledge and yield to His sovereignty, we glorify Him. That is what it means to glorify God.

At the cross every attribute of God was manifest as it had never been manifest before. The power of God, for example, was made visible on the cross. The kings of the earth and the rulers of the earth took counsel together against God and against His Christ. The terrible enmity of the carnal mind and the desperate wickedness of the human heart nailed Jesus to a cross. The fiendish hatred of Satan put forth its best effort. The world and Satan and every demon in the universe threw all the power they had at Christ, and He had the power to overcome it all. In death He broke every shackle, every dominance of sin, and every power of Satan forever. His graphic display of God's power thus glorified God.

The justice of God is seen in the cross in all its fullness. The wages of sin is death, and if God was going to redeem sinners, someone had to die for their sin. The penalty of the law had to be enforced, or God's justice would be compromised. Isaiah says that as Jesus hung there on the cross, "the Lord . . . caused the iniquity of us all to fall on Him" (Isaiah 53:6). Even though it meant the slaying of His beloved Son, God would not overlook justice. Thus by paying the highest price, Christ glorified God on the cross by displaying His justice in the greatest possible way — more so than if every member of the human race were to suffer in hell forever.

God's holiness was also manifest at the cross. Concerning His holiness, Habakkuk wrote that God is "of purer eyes than to behold evil, and [cannot] look on iniquity" (Habakkuk 1:13, KJV). Never did God so manifest His hatred for sin as in the suffering and death of His own Son. As Christ hung on the cross, bearing the sins of the world, God turned away from His only begotten Son in the midst of His suffering. Even though He loved Jesus Christ with an infinite love, His holiness could not tolerate looking on the sins of the world. That is why Jesus cried out in agony, "My God, My God, why hast thou forsaken Me?" (Matthew 27:46). All the cheerful obedience of the holy men of all ages is nothing in comparison with the offering of Christ Himself in order that every demand of God's holiness might be fully met. Through it, God was glorified.

God's faithfulness was displayed at the cross. From the beginning, He had promised the world a Savior. When Christ, the sinless One, was offered on the cross to receive the full and final wages of sin, God showed to all heaven and earth that He was faithful. Even though it cost Him His only Son, He went through with it. When we see that kind of faithfulness, we are seeing His glory.

There are many other attributes of God that were displayed in their fullness at the cross, but the one that stands above all the others is the attribute of love. "In this is love, not that we loved God, but that that He loved us and sent His Son to be the propitiation for our sins" (1 John 4:10). The human mind cannot comprehend the love that would cause God to permit His Son to die as an atonement for our sins. But He is glorified in the display of it.

"GOD WILL ALSO GLORIFY HIM"

In His third and final statement about glory, Jesus emphasized the truth that the Father and the Son were engaged in glorifying each other and that the greatest glory for the Son would be subsequent to His work on the cross. "If God is glorified in Him, God will also glorify Him in Himself, and will glorify Him immediately" (v. 32). There would be a certain glory in the cross, but the Father would not stop there. The resurrection, the ascension, the exaltation of Christ at the right hand of the Father, and the return of Christ in total glory would all be important aspects of the glory that would be His. Even today, His greatest glory is yet future.

The glory that was coming to Christ meant He had to leave the disciples. Therefore, Christ said to them, "Little children, I am with you a little while longer. You shall seek Me; and as I said to the Jews, I now say to you also, 'Where I am going, you cannot come' " (v. 33). Although His thoughts were on His glory and all the grandeur of it, He was also thinking about His eleven beloved disciples. He called them "little children" — an expression He probably would not have used if Judas had still been present.

What did He mean, "As I said to the Jews"? He was referring to several pronouncements of judgment He had made. In John 7:34, He told the Jews who sought to have Him seized, "You shall seek Me, and shall not find Me; and where I am, you cannot come." In John 8:21 he said again to the Jews, "I go away, and you shall seek Me, and shall die in your sin; where I am going, you cannot come." In 8:24, He added, "I said therefore to you, that you shall die in your sins; for unless you believe that I am He, you shall die in your sins."

It is significant that Jesus gave no such warning to His believing disciples. Although they would not be able at that time to follow Him where He was going, there was no danger that they would die in their sins. Jesus was going to the Father, and they would miss His physical nearness, especially in times of trial and problems. In fact, in Acts 1, as Jesus ascended into heaven, they just stood there, gazing longingly upward. They did not want Him to leave, and Jesus knew that. So here in John 13, He reasssured them that although His glory involved His leaving them for a time, He still cared for them. It was the introduction of a theme that would carry through the next few chapters.

Why did He tell them all this? Because He knew that, as true disciples, their concern was for His glory. He wanted them to share the expectation and excitement and anticipation of His coming glory. He wanted them to be preoccupied with thoughts of His glory.

A concern for God's glory, then, is one of the marks of a true disciple. It is the heart of the reason for our existence, a burning passion we inherit from our Lord Himself.

When Henry Martyn sailed for India, he said, "Let me burn out for God." Later, as he watched in a Hindu temple, he saw people prostrating themselves before images. He wrote in his diary, "This excited more horror in me than I can express." He wrote, "I could not endure existence if Jesus was not glorified, it would be hell to me." Once somebody said to him, "Why are you so preoccupied with His glory?" And he answered, "If someone plucks out your eyes, there's no saying *why* you feel pain, it is feeling — it is you. It is because I am one with Christ that I am so deeply wounded." Every genuine disciple knows something of that feeling.

AN UNFAILING LOVE FOR THE CHILDREN OF GOD

Not only is the committed disciple preoccupied with his Lord's glory, but also he is filled with His love. Perhaps this mark of the committed Christian is the most significant of all in terms of practical living as a sign that will distinguish us in the world.

Even though the disciples would no longer be able to rejoice in the visible presence of Jesus, they would still enjoy a full, rich experience of love, for they would have a depository of love in their own lives. In fact, love would be their primary distinguishing mark: "A new commandment I give to you, that you love one another, even as I have loved you, that you also love one another. By this all men will know that you are My disciples, if you have love for one another" (vv. 34-35). Those words of Christ had such a profound impact on the apostle John that he made them his life's message. He repeated the teaching in 1 John 3:11: "For this is the message which you have heard from the beginning, that we should love one another."

As believers in Christ, we have a new, God-given capacity to love. The love of Christ is "shed abroad in our hearts" (Romans 5:5, KJV), and Romans 13:8-10 tells us that love eliminates the necessity of a legal system. Because of love, we do not need to live by a set of rules and regulations. We do not need signs in our houses that say, "Don't bullwhip your wife"; "Don't smash your children with a hammer"; or, "Don't steal, kill, or bear false witness." Genuine love makes all the rules superfluous.

What kind of love marks a true disciple? Jesus said, "Love one another, even as I have loved you." That set the standard high, didn't it? Jesus' love is selfless, sacrificial, indiscriminate, understanding, and forgiving. Unless your love is like that, you have not fulfilled the new commandment.

If the church exhibited that kind of love, it would absolutely overwhelm the world. Unfortunately, that is not the way the professing church operates. There are factions, little groups, splits, and cliques. People gossip, backbite, talk, and criticize. The world looks, and it does not see much love. So there is no way for the world to know whether those who call themselves Christians are real or not.

One reason pseudo-Christian cults and false doctrines have so much influence today is that not many Christians are definitive disciples. It is often virtually impossible to distinguish a true disciple from a false one, for there is not a great deal of visible manifestation of God's love. Thus the world does not know to whom to go to find the truth. When the average person looks at the spectrum of "Christianity" and all that goes with it, he is baffled. Those around him who claim to be Christians seem to have no identifying marks, and, if anything, they often seem to be more lacking in love than in any other characteristic.

You will remember that in the first part of John 13, Jesus taught the disciples by washing their feet that the key to love is humility. Here is how closely love is tied to humility: If you do not have love, it is because you are proud. And God hates a proud heart. Those who are proud have no capacity for love. In Philippians 2:3-4, Paul says, "Do nothing from selfishness or empty conceit, but with humility of mind let each of you regard one another as more important than himself; do not merely look out for your own personal interests, but also for the interests of others." That is exactly what Jesus did, and how He taught His disciples to love.

How can we manifest visible love? First, we can admit it when we have wronged someone. If you are not willing to go to somebody you have wronged and make things right, the whole Body of Christ will be incapacitated because of your unwillingness to love.

Most of the bitterness within the visible church has nothing to do with doctrinal differences. It can be traced instead to a fundamental lack of love and to an unwillingness to accept the humility that love demands. A second way we can show love is by forgiving those who have wronged us — whether we are asked or not. No matter how serious the wrong you have suffered may be, love demands that you forgive it. Christ forgave those who had mocked Him, spit on Him, and then crucified Him. The wrongs we generally suffer are insignificant compared to what He suffered, and yet He was immediately willing to forgive.

Scripture is clear and unyielding on this principle of unconditional forgiveness. First Corinthians 6:1 says, "Does any one of you, when he has a case against his neighbor, dare to go to law before the unrighteous?" Apparently, some of the Corinthians were suing other believers for wrongs that had been committed against them.

Verse 7 of the passage says, "Actually, then, it is already a defeat for you, that you have lawsuits with one another. Why not rather be wronged? Why not rather be defrauded?" No verse in all of Scripture is more practical and demanding than that.

Do you really want to maintain a testimony of love in this world? Then accept whatever comes your way, praise the Lord, and let His love flow through you to the one who wronged you. That kind of love will confound the world.

Genuine love is costly, and the one who truly loves will have to sacrifice; but though you sacrifice in this world, you will gain immeasurably in the spiritual realm. And as you love others you will be displaying the most visible, practical, obvious mark of a true disciple.

AN UNSWERVING LOYALTY TO THE SON OF GOD

A third mark of the committed Christian is loyalty. It is more implied than expressed in the context of John 13. Nevertheless, it is included with a marvelous illustration of Peter, who faltered often but ultimately proved himself to be a genuinely committed believer and a true disciple. From him we learn a number of intensely practical principles that can make a difference in all our lives.

Discipleship is more than a promised loyalty. It must go beyond making a vow to God (which we tend to do glibly and frequently). Discipleship demands a practiced loyalty — an operating, functioning kind of loyalty that holds up under every kind of pressure.

All this talk about Jesus' going away must have deeply bothered Peter. He could not stand the thought of Jesus' leaving. Matthew 16:22-23 vividly shows how intensely Peter hated the thought of Jesus' impending death. Jesus had foretold His crucifixion and resurrection, and Peter, always the self-appointed spokesman for the disciples, took Jesus aside and began to rebuke Him. This was a stubborn, selfish attitude on the part of Peter, who did not want Jesus to be taken from him under any circumstances. Jesus "turned and said to Peter, 'Get behind Me, Satan! You are a stumbling block to Me; for you are not setting your mind on God's interests, but man's.'"

Jesus was completely aware of Peter's attitude, and in John 13 He took the opportunity to teach Peter a lesson about true loyalty:

> Simon Peter said to Him, "Lord, where are You going?"
> Jesus answered, "Where I go, you cannot follow Me now; but you shall follow later."

> Peter said to Him, "Lord, why can I not follow You right now? I will lay down my life for You."
>
> Jesus answered, "Will you lay down your life for Me? Truly, truly, I say to you, a cock shall not crow, until you deny Me three times."

>   (vv. 36-38)

Peter's heart was burning with love for Jesus. But though his love for Jesus was admirable, his boasting was foolish. His refusal to accept Jesus' words was merely stubborn pride. In essence, he was saying, "If all You're going to do is die, I will be happy to die with You." But he was speaking rashly, as a braggart. Perhaps he said it for the benefit of the other disciples, but he was saying it in the flesh. Worst of all, the message to Jesus was, "I know better than You."

You can imagine what a shock it was to Peter when Jesus predicted that he would deny Him that very night. In fact, through the rest of the dialogue, Peter — uncharacteristically — never said another word.

Nevertheless, we read in Matthew 26 that he repeated his boast later that evening in the garden. This time all the disciples joined with him in affirming that they would stay with Jesus, even if it meant dying. But just a short time later, when their lives seemed truly to be on the line, "all the disciples left Him and fled" (Matthew 26:56).

There was a huge gap in them between promised loyalty and practiced loyalty. Peter, who had so loudly boasted that he would stand by the Lord, failed miserably. Instead of giving his life for Jesus, he tried to save it by denying Him. And he did not do it in silence or by implication; he did it loudly, with cursing, and before many witnesses. Four things made Peter fail the test of loyalty.

HE BOASTED TOO MUCH

First, Peter was too proud to listen to what Jesus was trying to tell him, and too busy boasting. Luke 22:31-32 records Jesus' admonition to Peter: "Simon, Simon, behold, Satan has demanded permission to sift you like wheat; but I have prayed for you, that your faith may not fail; and you, when once you have turned again, strengthen your brothers." Implied in that warning was the prophecy that Peter would fail and that he would later repent of his failure.

But Peter missed the point. "Lord, with You I am ready to go both to prison and to death!" (v. 33). Reading his words, I think of 1 Kings 20:11: "Let not him who girds on his armor boast like him who takes it off." Peter should have waited to boast until after his trial.

It is dangerous to boast if you do not have anything to boast about. And it is especially dangerous to boast in yourself. Peter was boasting in his flesh, but actually he was not in a position to boast about anything.

HE PRAYED TOO LITTLE

Peter failed also because his praying was not what it should have been. First he was boasting when he should have been listening; and later that evening he slept when he should have been praying. Sleep is a good thing, but it is not a substitute for prayer. While Jesus was praying in agony in Gethsemane, Peter and the other disciples fell asleep. Luke 22:45-46 tells us that Jesus "came to the disciples and found them sleeping from sorrow, and said to them, 'Why are you sleeping? Rise and pray that you may not enter into temptation.' "

That rebuke must have made a profound impact on Peter, for many years later he wrote, "Be ye therefore sober, and watch unto prayer" (1 Peter 4:7, KJV). *Watch* means "stay alive," "stay awake," "stay alert." Peter's statement was not some kind of abstract, theological reasoning. It came out of his own experience.

HE ACTED TOO FAST

Another reason Peter failed the test of loyalty is that he was impetuous. Acting without thinking was a perennial problem in Peter's life. When a group of officers from the priests and Pharisees came into the garden to take Jesus, Peter grabbed a sword and cut off the high priest's slave's ear (Luke 22:50). Peter's motive, however, was selfishness, or perhaps fear or pride, but it was not loyalty. Jesus rebuked him for his action and healed the man's ear.

God's will is not always easy to accept, but those who are truly loyal will be sensitive to what it is. Peter might have thought he was helping the cause of God, but he was totally oblivious to all that God was doing in this, and his impetuous actions actually were getting in God's way and leading to his own fall.

HE FOLLOWED TOO FAR

A final reason for Peter's great failure is that he left Jesus' side and began to follow Him from a distance. Luke 22:54 says, "And having arrested Him, they led Him away, and brought Him to the

house of the high priest; but Peter was following at a distance."
That was perhaps the greatest disaster of all. Here was the logical
consequence of all of Peter's weaknesses: cowardice. He had fool-
ishly boasted of his willingness to die; now when he had that opportunity, for the first time in their relationship, Peter drifted from a
closeness with Jesus.

"And after they had kindled a fire in the middle of the courtyard
and had sat down together, Peter was sitting among them" (Luke
22:55). Suddenly he was sitting in the seat of the scornful. Luke
22:56 tells us that a servant girl recognized him as a follower of Jesus and pointed him out. Peter, who had bragged so forcefully of
his loyalty, now began to deny just as forcefully that he had ever
known Jesus.

There he was, within sight of the Lord, denying Him, even cursing and swearing that he had never known Him, according to
Matthew 26:72. When the cock crowed, Jesus turned around and
looked at Peter (Luke 22:61), and Peter remembered. He was so
ashamed that all he could do was run away and cry his heart out (v.
62).

What about your loyalty? What have you promised Jesus? That
you would love Him? That you would serve Him? That you would
be faithful, not deny Him, forsake sin, live or die for Him, or witness to your neighbor? How have you done? Did you boast too
much? Pray too little? Act too fast? Follow too far? How many
promises have you made to God and never kept?

It was not too late for Peter, and it is not too late for you. Peter
finally passed the test of loyalty. He finally preached, suffered, and
died for his Lord, just as he had promised. He proved himself to be
a genuine disciple. The first part of his story may be sad, but beginning with the book of Acts we see a different Peter.

Perhaps this is the most significant thing we learn from Peter:
God can turn a life around when it is finally yielded to Him. What
kind of a Christian are you? Are you everything you promised Jesus
Christ you would be when you first believed? Are you everything
you promised Christ you would be perhaps more recently, when
you reevaluated your life and recommitted it to Him? Are there visible, distinguishing marks that show you are a deeply committed
believer?

You may lack the marks of a committed Christian, but God can
transform you into a true disciple if you simply surrender and let
Him have your will. The life of a committed Christian may be costly, but it is the only kind of life that truly counts for eternity.

4

The Solution to a Troubled Heart

Those were dark hours that night before the Lord was betrayed, abused, tortured, and ultimately crucified. In a short time the world of the eleven disciples was going to collapse into unbelievable chaos. Jesus, for whom they had forsaken all, was leaving. Their beloved Master, whom they loved more than life, the One whom they had been willing to die for, was going away. Their sun was about to set at midday, and their whole world was going to fall in around them. In fact, the pains had already begun. The ramifications of all that Jesus had told them must have staggered their minds, and by chapter 14 they are undoubtedly bewildered, perplexed, confused, and filled with anxiety.

If you have ever lost a close loved one, you know what this kind of permanent separation is like. You can only imagine the feeling of losing One who was perfect, whose fellowship was completely pure, whose love was utterly flawless. It must have been an excruciating, horrifying pain.

And so in the beginning of John 14 Jesus anticipates the sorrow of their already breaking hearts, and He gives them comfort upon comfort. As we read Jesus' words in the first six verses we discover how deeply He cared for His disciples. He was about to be nailed to a cross, and He knew full well that He would soon bear the sins of every man who would ever live, be cursed with the curse of God, be forsaken by His own Father, and be spit on and mocked by evil

men. Any other man in that situation would have been in such a
state of uncontrollable agitation that he would never have been able
to focus his attention on the needs of others — but Jesus was
different.

Martin Luther called this passage "the best and most comforting
sermon that the Lord Christ delivered on earth, a treasure and a
jewel not to be purchased with the world's goods." These verses became the foundation of comfort for the disciples in the upper
room, and they are a source of comfort for us as well. If you ever
get to the point in your life where you think you have run out of es-
capes and there are no more places where you can rest, you will
find a tremendously soft, downy pillow in John 14:1-6:

> "Let not your heart be troubled; believe in God, believe also in
> Me. In My Father's house are many dwelling places; if it were not
> so, I would have told you; for I go to prepare a place for you. And
> if I go to prepare a place for you, I will come again, and receive
> you to Myself; that where I am, there you may be also. And you
> know the way where I am going."
>
> Thomas said to Him, "Lord, we do not know where You are go-
> ing, how do we know the way?"
>
> Jesus said to him, "I am the way, and the truth, and the life; no
> one comes to the Father, but through Me."

Here is Jesus Christ, fully divine but nevertheless totally human,
anticipating the most horrible kind of experience, yet completely
unconcerned at this point about His own experience and wholly absorbed in the needs of His eleven friends. Surely already feeling the
weight of the awful load of sin that He was about to bear, realizing
that He was about to taste the bitter cup of death for every man, He
nevertheless took a primary interest in the sorrows and the fears of
His apostles. As John writes in 13:1, "Having loved His own . . . He
loved them to the end."

If there is a single central message in Jesus' words, it is that the
basis of comfort is simple, trusting faith. If you are discontent, worried, anxious, bewildered, perplexed, confused, agitated, or otherwise in need of comfort, the reason is that you do not trust Him as
you should. If you really trust Christ, what do you have to worry
about? The reason the disciples were so stirred up is that they had
begun to focus on their problems and did not seem to be able to put
their trust in Christ. So in these verses He reminds them of the importance of trusting Him.

"Let not your heart be troubled" (v. 1) in the Greek language literally means, "Stop letting your hearts be troubled." He knew that they were already troubled. In fact, they were probably terrified. They were fully convinced that He was the Messiah, but the only real concept they had had of the Messiah was as an illustrious conqueror, a kind of superhero, a sovereign, ruling king. Their hopes had risen even higher just a week before, when Jesus had come riding into Jerusalem and everyone had thrown down palm branches and worshiped Him.

But even in the midst of that, Jesus had begun to talk about His dying (John 12:23-33). How could they reconcile that with His messiahship? And what about them? What kind of way was this to treat them? They had forsaken all and followed Him, and now He was going to forsake them. Not only that, but He was going to leave them in the midst of enemies who hated Him and them. Nothing seemed to fit. What good was a Messiah who was going to die? Why would He get their hopes up and then leave them stuck in the situation of being hated by all men? And where were their resources going to come from?

In addition, they had been informed by the Lord Himself that one of their own group would be the instrument of betrayal, and even that Peter, who was on the surface the strongest of all of them, would deny Him three times that very night. Everything seemed to be coming to an unbelievable climax.

Yet even though they were wavering, their love for Him was undiminished. Perhaps in the midst of their fears they were hoping against hope that He would do something to reverse what must have seemed to them like an impossible situation. Jesus, who could read their hearts like a billboard, knew exactly what they were thinking. He was touched with the feelings of their infirmities, and, in a sense, He shared their sorrows and their hurts. They could not feel His pain, but He could feel theirs.

Just as Isaiah had prophesied, "In all their affliction He was afflicted" (Isaiah 63:9). And, "The Lord [had] anointed [Him] to bring good news to the afflicted; . . . to bind up the brokenhearted, . . . [and] to comfort all who mourn" (61:1-2). He indeed knew "how to sustain the weary one with a word" (50:4).

It is interesting that all the time He was comforting them, He knew that they would scatter and forsake Him later that same night. Here was the agonizing Shepherd facing the cross, yet comforting the sheep who were going to be scattered and forsaken. "Let not your heart be troubled; believe in God, believe also in Me" (v. 1).

WE CAN TRUST HIS PRESENCE

What He was really saying was, "You can trust My presence." Jesus put Himself on an equal plane with God: "Believe in God; believe also in Me." In the Greek, that expression could be either imperative or indicative, for both forms are the same word. In other words, He might have been issuing a command: "Believe in God and also in Me" (imperative); or he might have been observing, "You believe in God, and you believe in Me" (indicative). There is no distinction in the Greek.

I believe, however, that what Jesus was actually saying was, "You believe in God, even though you cannot see Him. You also believe in Me. Keep believing. Your faith in Me must not be diminished just because you will not see Me. I will still be present with you." He wanted them to understand that even though He was leaving them physically, His presence would be with them spiritually. He would be leaving, but they would still have access to Him in the same way they had always had access to God.

Deuteronomy 31:6 says, "Be strong and courageous, do not be afraid or tremble at them, for the Lord your God is the one who goes with you. He will not fail you or forsake you." Such faith in the omnipresence of Jehovah was a basic tenet of the Jewish faith. Although they had never seen His form, all Jewish people believed implicitly that God was always present. Their history was proof of His eternal care and protection. They had full faith in an invisible God. Putting Himself on the same level as God, Jesus urged the disciples to trust Him even when He was not physically present.

Verse 1 has often been misapplied to make it seem that Jesus was speaking of saving faith. But He was not saying that they should believe in Him in order to be saved — they already believed in Him. He used a linear verb form, meaning, "Keep on trusting Me. Keep on trusting Me just as you are trusting God, even though I am not visible."

Let us face it, the disciples' faith was typified by Thomas. After the resurrection he heard that Christ was alive and had appeared to others. Thomas's response was, "Unless I shall see in His hands the imprint of the nails, and put my finger into the place of the nails, and put my hand into His side, I will not believe (John 20:25). Later, that was exactly the ground upon which Christ met Thomas. And when he saw for himself, he believed. The other disciples were not much different. They believed what they saw, and no more. That is the lowest level of faith.

In John 20:29, after Jesus showed Thomas the nail prints in His hands, He said, "Because you have seen Me, have you believed? Blessed are they who did not see, and yet believed." What He was trying to get across was that His visible presence was not nearly as significant as an understanding of His spiritual presence. He was there, laboring on their behalf, even when they could not see Him. It was a theme that colored everything He taught them: "For where two or three have gathered together in My name, there I am in their midst" (Matthew 18:20). "Lo, I am with you always, even to the end of the age" (Matthew 28:20). "I will never desert you, nor will I ever forsake you" (Hebrews 13:5).

Peter finally understood. Years later, he wrote in 1 Peter 1:8, speaking of Christ, "Though you have not seen Him, you love Him, and though you do not see Him now, but believe in Him, you greatly rejoice with joy inexpressible and full of glory." I have never seen Jesus Christ, but there is no one in existence in whom I believe more than I believe in Him. He is alive; He is real; I know Him; I sense His presence. You will never convince me that He is not alive. The Spirit of God witnesses in my heart continually that Jesus Christ lives. Although I cannot see Him, I trust Him.

We live with conflict, disappointment, and pain. We all experience hours of deep tragedy and times of severe trial, but He is with us. Whatever your trouble, whatever difficulty you are in, whatever anxiety or perplexity you have, just remember that the Lord Himself is there. In a way, it is better than if He were visible, because He is not hindered by the limitations of a physical body. He can be wherever we need Him. While He was here on earth, He could be in only one place at a time. Now He is available to all believers everywhere.

WE CAN TRUST HIS PROMISES

In addition to that reassurance, He gave the disciples wonderful promises. "In My Father's house are many dwelling places; if it were not so, I would have told you" (v. 2). That last phrase is filled with significance. He wanted them to know that He was not out to trick them and that He would not allow them to be deceived. They had many presuppositions and misconceptions that needed to be corrected, but their hope of eternity in heaven with Him was not one of those misconceptions. They believed, for example, that the Messiah would be a conquering monarch, and He had taught them that first He must be a suffering servant. Now, for the record, Jesus wanted to reassure them that their expectation of eternity in His kingdom was not a vain hope.

In fact, His leaving would be only to bring the fulfillment of that expectation to fruition: "I go to prepare a place for you" (v. 3). Can you imagine how it must have comforted them to realize for the first time *why* He was leaving? He was not going just to get away from them. He was going to get things *ready* for them.

It is important to note that He referred to heaven as "My Father's house." His favorite name for God was "My Father." Jesus, who had dwelt forever in the bosom of the Father, came forth so that He could reveal the Father and what the Father had been through all eternity. Now He would be glorified by death, and He was going back to full glory with the Father again in the Father's own house.

In the New Testament heaven is often called a country (emphasizing its vastness), a city (because of the large number of its inhabitants), a kingdom (because of its structure and order), and paradise (because of its beauty). But my favorite expression for heaven is this: "My Father's house." I remember that, as a child, if I went to visit relatives, or to camp, or away from home for any reason, it was an indescribable feeling of goodness to go back to my father's house. Even after I grew up and went to college, it was wonderful to have the opportunity to go home. There I was welcome. I was accepted. I was free to be myself. I could go right in, throw my coat off, kick off my shoes, flop into a chair, and relax. It was as much my home as my father's.

Heaven is like that. Going home to heaven will not be like going into a giant, unfamiliar place. We will be going home. It is our Father's house, but we are residents there, not guests. It is home, not some place where we are uncomfortable. It is home as home has never been.

The King James Version translates this verse, "In my Father's house are many mansions." For years, that translation has given many people the wrong idea. A number of our songs about heaven reflect the misconception that it is full of big mansions. Some seem to think that when you arrive in heaven you will be greeted by a heavenly real estate man, who will hand out little maps with instructions on how to get to the right mansion. And Peter will be at the gate with a golf cart to take you to your mansion.

But "dwelling places" is a more accurate translation than "mansions." In Jesus' culture, when a son was married, he seldom left his father's house. Instead, the father simply added another wing to the existing structure. If the father had more than one son, he would attach a new wing to the house for each son's new family. The new wings would enclose a patio, with the different families living around it.

That is the kind of arrangement Jesus was referring to. He was not talking about tenement rooms or mansions over the hillside but rather about a dwelling place that encompasses the complete family of God. We will dwell with God, not down the street from Him. We will have the same patio.

There will be enough room for everyone. There will be no over-crowding, no one turned away, no No Vacancy signs. Revelation 21:16 says, "And the city is laid out as a square, and its length is as great as the width; and he measured the city with the rod, fifteen hundred miles; its length and width and height are equal." Heaven, prepared uniquely for the redeemed to inhabit in glorified bodies, will be laid out like a cube.

Fifteen hundred miles *squared* is 2.25 million square miles. An area that size would cover almost half the continental United States. To give a point of reference, London is 140 square miles. If only the ground floor of heaven were populated at the same ratio as London, it could hold 1,000,000 million people — 30 times the cur-rent population of our world — in their unglorified bodies, and still have plenty of room to spare. Fifteen hundred miles *cubed* is 3,375,000,000 cubic miles, a volume larger than most of us can conceive.

Heaven is large, but fellowship in heaven is intimate. In Revela-tion 21:2-3, John writes, "And I saw the holy city, new Jerusalem, coming down out of heaven from God, made ready as a bride adorned for her husband. And I heard a loud voice from the throne, saying, 'Behold, the tabernacle of God is among men, and He shall dwell among them, and they shall be His people, and God Himself shall be among them.' " He is there, among His people, dwelling with them in unbroken and unhindered fellowship.

John goes on, "And He shall wipe away every tear from their eyes; and there shall no longer be any death; there shall no longer be any mourning, or crying, or pain; the first things have passed away" (v. 4). The Father takes care of all the hurts and the needs of the children in His house. There is no sense of need, no wanting anything, and no negative emotion.

I already feel bound to heaven. My Father is there; my Savior is there; my home is there; my name is there; my life is there; my af-fections are there; my heart is there; my inheritance is there; and my citizenship is there. Sometimes I wonder what I'm doing here!

Heaven will be an indescribably beautiful and glorious place. Imagine what it must be like — Jesus Christ, who created the uni-verse in a week, has been laboring for two millennia preparing heaven to be the habitation of His people. Revelation 21:18-22 de-scribes it.   4291

> And the material of the wall was jasper; and the city was pure
> gold, like clear glass. The foundation stones of the city wall were
> adorned with every kind of precious stone. The first foundation
> stone was jasper; the second, sapphire; the third, chalcedony; the
> fourth, emerald; the fifth, sardonyx; the sixth, sardius; the se-
> venth, chrysolite; the eighth, beryl; the ninth, topaz; the tenth,
> chrysoprase; the eleventh, jacinth; the twelfth, amethyst. And the
> twelve gates were twelve pearls; each one of the gates was a single
> pearl. And the street of the city was pure gold, like transparent
> glass. And I saw no temple in it, for the Lord God, the Almighty,
> and the Lamb, are its temple.

John goes on to write of how the glory of God will illuminate the city. Imagine the purest, brightest light flashing through the jewels in the walls of that fabulous city. Its gates are never shut (v. 25), yet nothing defiling can enter it. What a city it will be! Transparent gold, diamond walls, and light from the Lamb's glory will form a spectacle of dazzling beauty. And the Lord Jesus is preparing it especially for His own.

"If it were not so, I would have told you" (v. 2). He was saying, "Trust my promises! I've always told you the truth." He continued, "And if I go and prepare a place for you, I will come again, and re-ceive you to Myself; that where I am, there you may be also" (v. 3). What a reassurance this must have been to those frightened disci-ples that dark night! As surely as He was leaving, He would return in person, to receive them into the place He would prepare for them.

We can have complete confidence that He is coming back, al-though we do not know when. In fact, Jesus is anxious to return and claim His own. In John 17:24, He prays to the Father, "I desire that they also, whom Thou hast given Me, be with Me where I am, in order that they may behold My glory." Jesus wants us with Him as much as we want to be with Him.

He is coming back. That subject is on the lips of Christians all over the world. It always has been, but today there seems to be a heightened awareness, a deepening anticipation that Jesus is com-ing. The stage is completely set for His return. Jesus could well come in this generation. In fact, He could come today. But even if He does not, we know He will someday. He desires it as much as we do.

WE CAN TRUST HIS PERSON

The disciples must have been completely bewildered when Jesus, speaking of His departure, added, "And you know the way where I am going" (v. 4). Up to this point, they had completely resisted any idea of His leaving. Now they were not certain of anything. Thomas probably spoke for the rest when he said, "Lord, we do not know where You are going, how do we know the way?" (v. 5).

Thomas was saying, "Our knowledge stops at death. How can we go to the Father unless we die? You are going to die and go somewhere, but we do not know what goes on after death. We do not have any maps that show us how to get to the Father after You die." It was a good question.

Jesus' response was profound: "I am the way, and the truth, and the life; no one comes to the Father, but through Me" (v. 6). In other words, "You do not need to know how to get there; I am coming to get you." It was a reaffirmation of all He had just promised them. It was a beautiful promise.

Have you ever been driving in an unfamiliar town and stopped to ask directions? If your experience was like mine, you have probably had someone give you a complex set of directions that you could not possibly understand. How much better it would have been for the person to say, "Follow me; I'll take you there." That is what Jesus does. He does not *show* us the direction to the Father's house, He *carries* us there. That is why death for the Christian is such a glorious experience. Whether we die, or whether He takes us in the rapture, we know we can trust Him to take us to the Father's house.

August Toplady, who wrote "Rock of Ages," died in London at the age of thirty-eight. When death drew near he said, "It is my dying vow that these great and glorious truths which the Lord in rich mercy has given me to believe and enabled me to preach are now brought into practical and heartfelt experience. They are the very joy and support of my soul. The comfort flowing from them carries me far above the things of time and sin." Then he said, "Had I wings like a dove I would fly away to the bosom of God and be at rest." About an hour before he died he seemed to awaken from a gentle slumber, and his last words were, "Oh! What delight! Who can fathom the joys of heaven! I know it cannot be long now until my Savior will come for me." And then bursting into a flood of tears he said, "All is light, light, light, the brightness of His own glory. Oh come Lord Jesus, come. Come quickly!" And he closed his eyes.

"Trust Me," Jesus says. "You don't need a map; I'm the way, the truth, and the life. I am the way to the Father. I am the truth, whether in this world or the world to come. I am the life that is eternal."

Christ is everything a man needs. Everything that Adam lost we may regain in Jesus Christ. We can trust His presence, His promises, and His person, for He is the way, the truth, and the life. I know of no greater comfort in all the world than that.

5
Jesus Is God

The strategic importance of those final hours in the upper room with the eleven disciples cannot be overstated. All Jesus' instructions to them that night, His warnings, His teaching, His commandments, His promises, and His revelation were calculated to build them up and brace them for the trauma they were about to experience. It was essential that Jesus prepare them for the shock of His death. The news of His leaving was a tremendous blow to them, and their hearts were already deeply troubled. They had put all their faith in Him, and they loved Him more than life itself. Their faith might have been seriously damaged if they had seen Him die without having heard what He had to say in those few remaining hours.

The disciples had been witnesses to amazing events in the three brief years of Jesus' ministry. He had cast out demons, healed people with every conceivable sickness, and even raised people from the dead. He had demonstrated His power over every adversary, and in every situation where it seemed He was threatened, He had come forth the victor. He had successfully countered every argument, answered every question, resisted every temptation, and confounded every enemy. But now He was predicting His own death at the hands of wicked men.

The confused disciples did not understand how Messiah could become a victim of the people. It did not fit their concept of what His mission would be. Not only that, but they had also become increasingly aware that Jesus was the incarnation of God. They thought of Him as invincible, omniscient, and devoid of any kind of weakness. Now they were understandably confused. Why would He die? How could He die? Who could defeat Him? How could anyone else ever accept Him as Messiah if He died? Did this mean that all they had lived for the past three years was in vain? And most crucial, did it mean that Jesus was not who they thought?

Sensing the nagging questions of their troubled hearts, Jesus continued His ministry of comfort to them by reaffirming His deity:

> "If you had known Me, you would have known My Father also; from now on you know Him, and have seen Him."
>
> Philip said to Him, "Lord, show us the Father, and it is enough for us."
>
> Jesus said to him, "Have I been so long with you, and yet you have not come to know Me, Philip? He who has seen Me has seen the Father; how do you say, 'Show us the Father'? Do you not believe that I am in the Father, and the Father is in Me? The words that I say to you I do not speak on My own initiative, but the Father abiding in Me does His works. Believe Me that I am in the Father, and the Father in Me; otherwise believe on account of the works themselves. Truly, truly, I say to you, he who believes in Me, the works that I do shall he do also; and greater works than these shall he do; because I go to the Father. And whatever you ask in My name, that will I do, that the Father may be glorified in the Son. If you ask Me anything in My name, I will do it."
>
> (John 14:7-14)

The implications of Jesus' words in these few verses are overwhelming. The fact that He claims to be God is profound enough. But then He adds both a guarantee that believers in Him will have power to do even greater works than He has done and an assertion that if they ask anything in His name He will do it. His words are monumental in declaring not only who He is but also what he intends to do in and for those who belong to Him.

Notice that our Lord was making three momentous revelations to His disciples.

THE REVELATION OF HIS PERSON

The first of those was the revelation of His person. Only a few days before, when Jesus had entered Jerusalem on the back of a donkey to shouts of "Hosanna," there was no question in their minds about who He was. Now they were not sure. In their hearts

they were asking questions about Him that had been answered before; consequently, Jesus reiterated to them who He really was by
revealing His person to them in fresh and unmistakable terminology: "He who has seen Me has seen the Father" (v. 9). "I am in the
Father, and the Father is in Me" (v. 10).

What did He reveal to them about Himself? One thing: that He is
God. They had heard His claims of deity before, and they had witnessed the proof of it in His works. He had said in verse 6 that He
was the way to God, the truth about God, and the very life of God.
He went a step further in verses 7-10 and said in unequivocal terms
that He *is* God. His words must have been staggering, because the
claim is so tremendous.

Yet it cannot be dismissed. The single, central, most important issue about Jesus is the question of His deity. Everyone who studies
about Jesus must confront the issue, because of His claims to be
God. C. S. Lewis has observed that "the one thing we must not say"
about Jesus is that He is a "great moral teacher" but not God:

> A man who was merely a man and said the sort of things Jesus
> said would not be a great moral teacher. He would either be a lun-
> atic — on a level with the man who says he is a poached egg — or
> else he would be the Devil of Hell. You must make your choice.
> Either this man was, and is, the Son of God: or else a madman or
> something worse.[1]

Sabellius, a second-century heretic and the forerunner of the Unitarians, taught that Jesus was only a radiation, a manifestation of
God. But He is not a manifestation of God; He is God *manifest.*
There is a significant difference. Jesus is uniquely one with, but distinct from, the Father — God manifest in human flesh.

Here in John 14 Jesus makes the simple, undisguised claim that
He is no less than God. He had told them many times in the past
that He proceeded from the Father. Now, in verse 4, He implies
that they should have understood: "You know the way where I am
going." They *should* have known at least that He was going to be
with the Father. But His words leave them scratching their heads,
and Thomas asks for an explanation. Jesus' answer is simply, "I am
the way, and the truth, and the life; no one comes to the Father, but
through Me" (v. 6).

It was a claim of divine authority. In other words, "If you know
Me, you know the way to get where I am going. I am going to the
Father, and I will take you." He reinforced that claim with a mild

1. *Mere Christianity* (New York: Macmillan, 1960), p. 41.

rebuke for their unbelief and a reassurance that they were as secure in their relationship with the Father as they were in their relationship with the Son: "If you had known Me, you would have known My Father also; from now on you know Him, and have seen Him" (v. 7).

In a sense, the disciples did not know Jesus at all. If they had really known Him as they thought, they would not have been worried about where the Father was.

They had some knowledge of who Jesus was. They had declared that He was the Messiah, the Anointed One of God. Peter had even made the statement that He was the Son of the living God. They were close to grasping fully the truth of His deity, and they were beginning to understand the meaning of it. Nevertheless, they were still confused, so Jesus stated the truth in the clearest possible language, terms that they could not possibly miss: "If you had known Me, you would have known My Father also; from now on you know Him, and have seen him. . . . He who has seen Me has seen the Father. . . . I am in the Father, and the Father is in Me" (vv. 7-10).

In other words, Jesus was saying, "If you really knew me in depth, you would know the Father also. Your confusion about the Father means that there must be some gaps in your knowledge of Me." If they had really seen Jesus fully as God, they would not have had fears, doubts, and questions about who the Father was and how to get to Him.

Remember, Jesus' words were meant to comfort them. They knew He loved them. He wanted them to know that God cared for them in the same way, because He and the Father are one. To have a relationship with one is to have a relationship with the other. That is an important, eternal principle. If you reject the Son, you have rejected the Father; and if you receive the Son you have received the Father. The apostle John grasped this in its fullness, and it became a theme of his ministry. Years later, he wrote, "Whoever denies the Son does not have the Father; the one who confesses the Son has the Father also" (1 John 2:23).

But it appears that none of the disciples immediately understood the full import of what Jesus was telling them. His words "From now on you know Him, and have seen Him" (v. 7) were more a prediction than a proclamation. "From now on" did not mean "from this precise moment on," for they did not yet grasp what He was saying. In fact, in the very next verse Philip proved he still did not know who Jesus was in the full sense. Similarly, His words "You know Him, and have seen Him" did not mean that the opening of their understanding about God had actually been accomplished.

Instead, using the idiom of His day, Jesus spoke in the present tense to signify the ultimate certainty of what He was saying. The message to the disciples was, "Starting now, you are going to begin to understand." Through the events of the next forty days — the death of Jesus Christ, His resurrection, His ascension, and the coming of the Holy Spirit — they would come to understand more fully about Jesus' person and His relationship to the Father.

And that is exactly what happened. Thomas, for example, had doubted the resurrection even after hearing eyewitness testimony, but when he saw Christ, finally it all fell into place, and he understood who Jesus was. He looked at the risen Jesus and said, "My Lord and my God!" (John 20:28).

Philip's request in verse 8, "Lord, show us the Father, and it is enough for us," proves that at the time of the upper room discourse in John 14 the disciples did not yet see the full truth of who Jesus is. It was a shallow, faithless, ignorant thing to say, and it revealed his lack of understanding. His knowledge of Christ was incomplete, and his knowlege of God was incomplete. So he did what people have done throughout history: he asked to see.

Philip was trying to walk by sight rather than by faith. It wasn't enough for him to believe; he wanted to *see* something. It could be that he remembered the account of Exodus 33, when Moses was tucked in a rock and he saw the afterglow of God's glory pass by. Or maybe he recalled the words of Isaiah 40:5: "Then the glory of the Lord will be revealed, and all flesh will see it together."

Perhaps, but I do not think he was a biblical scholar at all. I think he was a faithless disciple who wanted sight to substitute for faith. We can understand his feelings. It would be a great deal easier for the disciples to tolerate Jesus' departure if they could first have a glimpse of the Father, just to make certain Jesus really knew where He was going. It would be much easier to cling to Jesus' promise that He would come again to get them, if God could come and confirm it. If Jesus could to that, there would be no doubt about whether His claims where real. God Himself would be a guarantee that Jesus' pledge was secure.

It was not the first time Jesus had dealt with this question. Earlier (John 8:19) some unbelieving Jews had asked, "Where is Your Father?" Jesus had answered, "You know neither Me, nor My Father; if you knew Me, you would know My Father also."

Philip's question revealed his lack of faith, and Jesus gave him the same answer He had given the unbelieving Jews: "Have I been so long with you, and yet you have not come to know Me, Philip? He who has seen Me has seen the Father; how do you say, 'Show us the

Father'?" (v. 9). That was, of course, a rebuke to Philip, but I believe there was also pathos in the voice of Jesus. Can you imagine the heartbreak of Jesus, after He had poured His life into those twelve men for three years, to know that one of them was a traitor, one of them a swearing denier, and the ten that were left were of little faith? It was the night before His death, and still they did not really know who He was.

Imagine Philip, standing there staring Christ in the face and asking Him to show him God. Jesus' answer to him was, "Open your eyes. You've been looking at Me for three years." They who had seen Jesus had seen the visible manifestation of God. The writer of Hebrews says, "[Jesus Christ] is the radiance of His glory and the exact representation of His nature," or, as the King James Version puts it, "the express image of His person" (Hebrews 1:3). In Colossians, the apostle Paul writes, "He is the image of the invisible God," and, "In Him all the fullness of Deity dwells in bodily form" (1:15; 2:9). Jesus is God.

It is easy to see how unbelievers might say what Philip did. But for him to ask to see the Father as proof of Jesus' claims does not make much sense. He and the other disciples had seen Jesus' works and heard His words for three years.

Anyone who has ever discipled another Christian must know something of what Jesus felt in the face of Philip's frustrating unbelief. But Jesus was not discouraged. He had gone as far as He could with the disciples, and now He was ready to turn them over to the Holy Spirit. That is a good principle to apply in discipleship.

Jesus' answer might not have been especially satisfying to Philip, but it was exactly what Philip needed. Jesus did not do any miracles for him or give him any great display of power; He simply commanded him to believe. "Do you not believe that I am in the Father, and the Father is in Me? The words that I say to you I do not speak on My own initiative, but the Father abiding in Me does His works. Believe Me that I am in the Father, and the Father in Me; otherwise believe on account of the works themselves" (vv. 10-11). Philip asked for sight; Jesus told him to seek faith instead.

Christianity is all about believing. If you think the height of spirituality is to see miracles, to hear the voice of God booming out of the ceiling, or to experience some kind of supernatural phenomenon, you do not have a clue as to what believing God is all about. Satan can duplicate all those things in counterfeit. If you want manifestations of supernatural power, you can get them at a seance.

Christianity is walking by faith, not sight. I have never seen Jesus, never had a vision, never seen angelic hosts, never heard heavenly voices, and never been carried into the third heaven. Yet my spiritual eyes can see things that my physical eyes could never even conceive of. I do not want visions, miracles, and strange phenomena. I do not want superfantastic, ecstatic things to happen; I want one thing — I want what the disciples prayed for in Luke 17:5: "Increase our faith."

Faith is not as one little boy described it: "Believing in something you know ain't so." In fact, faith is just the opposite — believing in something you know *is* so. Genuine faith has an essential basis in fact.

The disciples certainly had a factual basis for their faith, and Jesus reemphasized that to Philip: "The words that I say to you I do not speak on My own initiative, but the Father abiding in Me does His works. Believe Me that I am in the Father, and the Father in Me; otherwise believe on account of the works themselves" (vv. 10-11). If Philip and the others had truly been listening for the past three years, if they had really paid attention to the works Jesus did, they would not have doubted now.

There is always danger of doubting in the darkness things that we have seen clearly in the light. That is what the disciples were doing. During the three years of Jesus' earthly ministry they had repeatedly heard and seen proof that He was God incarnate. Now their faith was wavering, in spite of the solid, factual foundation upon which it was built. They had heard all His claims, all His teachings, all His insights probing into hidden truths, all His words revealing a supernatural knowledge of the human heart. He had answered questions that they had asked not with their lips, but in their hearts. And if His words were not sufficient proof, they had seen His works — His miracles and His sinless life.

Philip's request to see God, then, was a gross display of unbelief. He did not need to see anything; Jesus had proved that He is God. What more could He show them? He was God manifest. They had heard His words, beheld His works, witnessed His glory, observed His perfection, and experienced His love for them. How could they ask such a question now?

And so He reaffirmed to them the tremendous revelation that He is God. If they could grasp that truth, they could rest easy, knowing they were secure.

THE REVELATION OF HIS POWER

Next, He revealed to them the incredible resource of power they had available to them through Him. "Truly, truly, I say to you, he who believes in Me, the works that I do shall he do also; and greater works than these shall he do; because I go to the Father (v. 12). Christians over the centuries have wondered at the richness of such a promise. What does it mean? How could anyone do greater works than Jesus had done? He had healed people blind from birth, cast out the most powerful demons, and even raised a man from the dead after four days. What could possibly be greater than that?

The key to understanding this promise is in the last phrase of verse 12: "because I go unto the Father." When Jesus went to the Father, He sent the Holy Spirit. He completely transformed the disciples from a fearful group of timid individuals to a collective force that reached the world with the gospel. The impact of their preaching exceeded even the impact of Jesus' preaching during His lifetime. Jesus had never preached outside Palestine. Within His lifetime Europe had never received the word of the gospel. But under the ministry of the disciples the gospel began to spread, and it is still spreading today. The disciples' works were greater than His, not in power, but in scope. You see, through the indwelling Holy Spirit, each one of those disciples had access to power in dimensions they did not have even with the physical presence of Christ.

The disciples undoubtedly thought that without Christ they would be reduced to nothing. He was the source of their strength. How could they have power without Him? His promise was meant to ease those fears. If they felt secure in His presence, they would be even more secure, more powerful, more capable if He returned to the Father and sent the Holy Spirit.

The disciples had power to work great miracles — not greater than Christ's in power, but perhaps greater than His in scope. Acts 5 says that "at the hands of the apostles many signs and wonders were taking place among the people. . . . They even carried the sick out on the streets, and laid them on cots and pallets, so that when Peter came by, at least his shadow might fall on any one of them" (vv. 12, 15).

In Acts 2, Peter preaches, and three thousand people are saved. That never happened during the ministry of Jesus. He never saw widespread revival. The gospel never went to the Gentiles in the time of Jesus, but through the works of His apostles, conversions took place everywhere.

And after all, the greatest spiritual miracle that God can perform is salvation. Every time we introduce someone to Jesus Christ, we are literally involved in the new birth; we are doing the greatest possible work that can be done. How exciting it is to be able to be involved in what God is doing spiritually and to do things greater than even Jesus saw in His own day!

THE REVELATION OF HIS PROMISE

Finally, Jesus gave them a promise meant to ease the grief they felt at His leaving: "And whatever you ask in My name, that will I do, that the Father may be glorified in the Son. If you ask Me anything in My name, I will do it" (vv. 13-14).

Jesus had fed them. He had helped them catch their fish. On one occasion He had even provided their tax money out of the mouth of a fish. He had supplied all their needs, but now He was leaving, and they must have wondered, *How are we going to get a job? How are we going to fit back into society? What will we do without Him?*

They had left everything and were completely without resources. Without Jesus, they would be all alone in a hostile world. Yet, He assured them, they did not need to worry about any of their needs. The gap between Him and them would be closed instantly as they prayed. Even though He would be absent, they would have access to all His supplies.

That promise was not carte blanche for every whim of the flesh. There was a qualifying statement repeated twice. Jesus did not say, "I'll give you anything you ask for," but rather, "I'll do what you ask *in My name.*" That does not mean that we can simply tack "in Jesus' name amen" to the end of our prayers and expect an answer. Jesus was not speaking of a formula or abracadabra to use to get wishes granted.

The name of Jesus stands for all that He is. Throughout Scripture, God's names are the same as His attributes. When Isaiah prophesied that Messiah would be called "Wonderful Counselor, Mighty God, Eternal Father, Prince of Peace" (9:6), he was not giving actual names, but rather an overview of Messiah's character. "I AM THAT I AM," the name revealed to Moses in Exodus 3:14 (KJV), is as much an affirmation of God's eternal nature as it is a name by which He is to be called.

Therefore, praying in the name of Jesus is more than merely mentioning His name in a prayer. If we truly pray in Jesus' name, we can pray only for that which is consistent with His perfect character and for that which will bring glory to Him. It implies an acknowledgment of all that He has done and a submission to His will.

What it really means is that when we pray, we should pray as if Jesus Christ Himself were doing the asking. We approach the throne of the Father in full identification with the Son, seeking only what He would seek. When we pray with that perspective, we begin to pray for the things that really matter and eliminate selfish requests.

His promise when we pray that way is, "I will do it" (v. 14). That is a guarantee that within His will we cannot lack anything! His concern for His own transcends all circumstances, so that "neither death, nor life, nor angels, nor principalities, nor things present, nor things to come, nor powers, nor height, nor depth, nor any other created thing, shall be able to separate us from the love of God which is in Christ Jesus our Lord" (Romans 8:38-39).

That was the heart of Jesus' message of comfort to His terrified disciples, and it must have been tremendously reassuring to the disciples to hear those words and ponder them. In the midst of the collapse of their dreams and hopes, He gave them Himself as a rock to which they could cling and under which they could seek shelter.

He cares no less for those who are His disciples today. His promises are still valid, His power has not diminished, and His person is unchanging. We do not have the benefit of His physical presence, but we have His Spirit. And although we cannot see Jesus, we can sense His love for us as the Spirit sheds it abroad in our hearts. In many ways, we know Him better than if we knew Him from His mere physical presence. As Peter wrote, "Though you have not seen Him, you love Him, and though you do not see Him now, but believe in Him, you greatly rejoice with joy inexpressible and full of glory" (1 Peter 1:8).

What a thrill it is to experience His love in this way, and what a comfort to know that He is God and that He cares for us!

6

The Coming of the Comforter

You cannot study the New Testament long without seeing that there is a dichotomy between what we are responsible to do as Christians and what has already been done on our behalf. To understand the distinction is to get a grip on the basics of our faith.

On the one hand, we are told repeatedly in Scripture how we are to live, act, think, and speak. We are enjoined to be this or to commit ourselves to that. We are informed about what we are to do, at what point we are to commit ourselves, and for what tasks we are to separate ourselves. All these matters are essential to our faith.

But on the other hand, much of the New Testament emphasizes what Christ has already done for us. We are told that we are called, justified, sanctified, and kept in the faith through no effort of our own. We learn that Christ and the Holy Spirit are continually interceding on our behalf. And we discover that we are the recipients of an inheritance that cannot be measured in human terms.

Most of Jesus' final discourse to His disciples consisted not of commandments they were responsible to obey but rather of promises of what He would do on their behalf. John 14:15-26 is the heart of His message of comfort. Here, Jesus gives His disciples the promise that after His departure, the Holy Spirit would come in His place:

> "If you love Me, you will keep My commandments. And I will ask the Father, and He will give you another Helper, that He may be with you forever; that is the Spirit of truth, whom the world cannot receive, because it does not behold Him or know Him, but

you know Him because He abides with you, and will be in you.

"I will not leave you as orphans; I will come to you. After a little while the world will behold Me no more; but you will behold Me; because I live, you shall live also. In that day you shall know that I am in My Father, and you in Me, and I in you.

"He who has My commandments and keeps them, he it is who loves Me; and he who loves Me shall be loved by My Father, and I will love him, and will disclose Myself to him."

Judas (not Iscariot) said to Him, "Lord, what then has happened that You are going to disclose Yourself to us, and not to the world?"

Jesus answered and said to him, "If anyone loves Me, he will keep My word; and My Father will love him, and We will come to him, and make Our abode with him. He who does not love Me does not keep My words; and the word which you hear is not Mine, but the Father's who sent Me. These things I have spoken to you, while abiding with you. But the Helper, the Holy Spirit, whom the Father will send in My name, He will teach you all things, and bring to your remembrance all that I said to you."

The promises Jesus makes in this brief passage are staggering. To whom are they made? In context, Jesus is speaking to His eleven disciples, but the scope of His promises is broader than that. Verse 15 says, "If you love Me, you will keep My commandments." Implied in that statement is the corollary that the promises that follow apply to all those who love Jesus Christ. Thus they apply to all believers in Christ, those whose love is marked out by their obedience.

We cannot miss Jesus' clear statement here that the proof of genuine love for Him is obedience to His commandments. The New Testament repeats this truth a number of times. Verse 21 says, "He who has My commandments and keeps them, he it is who loves Me; and he who loves Me shall be loved by My Father, and I will love him, and will disclose Myself to him." Verses 23-24 repeat the same truth: "If anyone loves Me, he will keep My word. . . . He who does not love Me does not keep My words."

Love for Christ is not sentimentalism or a sickly pseudospiritual impression, and it does not result in mere lip service. Real love for Him is demonstrated by an active, eager, joyful, responsive obedience to His commandments. What you *say* about your love for Him is relatively unimportant. What counts is that you demonstrate your love for Him by how you live your life. Discipleship is not singing songs and saying nice things. True discipleship is obedience.

The Lord extends a number of promises to those who are obedient. Those promises are for all disciples in all ages. They are in the category of things that have been accomplished on our behalf without effort on our part. All are tied to the coming of the Holy Spirit — the Comforter, Teacher, and Helper who ministered to the disciples when Jesus left. Together, the promises constitute a legacy for all those who love Him.

THE INDWELLING SPIRIT

The promise of the Holy Spirit was the culmination of all that Jesus had to say to comfort those eleven troubled men. In that hour of turmoil, they feared being left alone. Jesus assured them that they would not be left to fend for themselves but would have a supernatural Helper (cf. v. 16). The Greek word for *helper* is *parakletos*, which literally means "one who is called *(kaleo)* alongside *(para)*." We sometimes use the term *Paraclete* in English. The King James Version translates it "Comforter," which is one of the meanings of the word. Jesus is saying, "I am going to send a Helper, a Comforter — one to stand alongside you."

The Greek word translated "another" is crucial to an understanding of Jesus' meaning. The Greek language, with all its complexities, is much more precise than English. The Greeks had two words that meant "another." One was *heteros,* which means "another kind," as in, "This wrench doesn't fit; bring me another one." *Allos* also means "another," but it means "another of the same kind," as in, "I enjoyed that sandwich; I think I'll have another."

Allos is the word Jesus used to describe the Holy Spirit: "another *[allos]* Helper." In effect, He is saying, "I am sending you One of exactly the same essence as Myself." The disciples would have known His meaning immediately. He was not sending back just any old helper but One exactly like Himself, with the same compassion, the same attributes of deity, and the same love for them.

Jesus had been their Paraclete for three years. He had helped them, had comforted them, and had walked alongside them. Now they would have another Helper — One exactly like Jesus — to minister to them as He had.

The Holy Spirit is not just a mystical power. He is a person as much as Jesus is a person. He is not a floating fog or ghostlike emanation. It is unfortunate that the King James translators used the term *Ghost* instead of *Spirit.* For generations people have had the idea that the Holy Spirit is something like Casper. He is not a ghost, but a person.

All believers have two Paracletes — the Spirit of God within us and Christ at the right hand of the Father in heaven. First John 2:1

says, "My little children, I am writing these things to you that you may not sin. And if anyone sins, we have an Advocate with the Father, Jesus Christ the righteous." The word translated "Advocate" in that verse is *parakletos.*

You can imagine that the disciples must have been greatly encouraged and comforted to hear Jesus say that He would send another Helper like Him to minister to them in His place when He left. As One who is the exact essence of Him, the Holy Spirit would be a perfect substitute for the familiar presence of Jesus.

But Jesus' promise extended beyond that. His next words beautifully culminated the message of comfort: "that He may be with you forever" (v. 16). Not only would the Holy Spirit come to dwell with them, He would never leave. Once the Spirit of God resides within a person, He is there forever.

In Luke 11:13, Jesus tells His disciples that the Father will give them the Holy Spirit if they ask. Yet here in John 14, before they can even ask, He asks in their behalf. That is a good picture of how our prayers operate. The Lord knows what we have need of before we even ask. I am sure that often, before we get our prayers organized, Jesus Christ has already asked in our behalf for what we need. That is part of His ministry of advocacy and intercession.

SPIRITUAL PERCEPTION

Notice that the Spirit is called "the Spirit of truth" (v. l7). He is both the essence of truth, because He is God, and the One who guides us into truth. Apart from Him, men cannot know or understand truth. In fact, unsaved men do not recognize the Spirit or His work, and that is as Jesus said it would be: "The world cannot receive [the Spirit of Truth], because it does not behold Him or know Him" (v. 17). If the world did not recognize the first Comforter, Jesus, you cannot expect it to recognize the second One, who is exactly like the first.

Unsaved men have no facility for spiritual perception. They have no way to see the working of the power of the Holy Spirit. When the academic minds of Jesus' day came to their conclusion about who He was, their astute, reasoned, theological pronouncement was that He was from the devil (Matthew 12:24) — and that came after years of studying His ministry. It showed graphically the spiritual capacity of unregenerate man. Given all the facts, he will invariably conclude the wrong thing.

In 1 Corinthians 2:12-14, the apostle Paul writes:

> Now we have received, not the spirit of the world, but the Spirit who is from God, that we might know the things freely given to us by God, which things we also speak, not in words taught by human wisdom, but in those taught by the Spirit, combining spiritual thoughts with spiritual words. But a natural man does not accept the things of the Spirit of God; for they are foolishness to him, and he cannot understand them, because they are spiritually appraised.

In other words, the only way a man can understand the things of God is to have the Spirit of God. The natural man cannot understand the Holy Spirit's work.

In fact, in John 8:44-45, 47, Jesus indicts the Jewish leaders:

> You are of your father the devil, and you want to do the desires of your father. He was a murderer from the beginning, and does not stand in the truth, because there is no truth in him. Whenever he speaks a lie, he speaks from his own nature; for he is a liar, and the father of lies. But because I speak the truth, you do not believe Me. . . . He who is of God hears the words of God; for this reason you do not hear them, because you are not of God.

All unsaved men, they had no capacity to comprehend the truth of God.

Consequently, Jesus told His disciples that when the Holy Spirit came, the world would not get the message any more than it believed Him when He came. And He was right. In Acts 2, when the Holy Spirit came on the day of Pentecost, the unbelievers who witnessed the manifestation thought the disciples were drunk. The Holy Spirit was just as foreign to the stubborn, rejecting world as Jesus had been.

When I first studied John 14, I was puzzled about why in this context Jesus told the disciples that the world would not respond to the Holy Spirit. Then it dawned on me that with all the promises that Jesus was giving the disciples, they might have succumbed to overconfidence. He had told them that they would do greater things than even He had done (v. 12), and He had promised to answer every prayer they asked (v. 14). They might have been feeling invincible. If they had entered the world to proclaim the gospel without knowing that the world would not understand, they might have been totally deflated when they encountered opposition from the world. Therefore, in this passage of John, Jesus tries to temper their enthusiasm.

The Eternal Union with God

At the end of verse 17, our Lord reveals a classic dispensational truth: "But you know Him because He abides with you, and will be in you." They knew of the ministry of God's Spirit from the Old Testament. In the Old Testament economy the Spirit of God sometimes came upon people for a certain service, and after it was accomplished, He departed. The Spirit of God came on Saul, Azariah, and Isaiah, for example. At Jesus' baptism the Spirit had descended on Him like a dove. The disciples were thus not ignorant of the ministry of the Spirit.

But notice Jesus' words: "He abides with you, *and will be in you*" (v. 17, emphasis added). The Holy Spirit would not just be present with them; He would indwell them, and the verb tense in the Greek indicates that it would be a permanent, uninterrupted residence. That had never happened in the Old Testament age.

Scripture had prophesied this in Ezekiel 37:14: "And I will put My Spirit within you, and you will come to life." That promise actually had reference to the nation of Israel in the Kingdom age, but it is prefigured in the church age.

What a privilege it is in the grace of God that He would plant His very essence in us. We have a supernatural helper, not just *with*, but *in* every one of us. Every moment of our existence throughout all eternity, we have the presence of the Holy Spirit within.

The Presence of Christ

Our Lord expands the promise in verses 18-19: "I will not leave you as orphans; I will come to you. After a little while the world will behold Me no more; but you will behold Me." This is the picture of a dying father. He would literally die before another day had passed, and He wanted to reassure them that they could nevertheless count on His presence after that.

There are at least two elements involved in this promise. For one thing, He was guaranteeing them that He would rise from the dead. His dying on the cross would not be the end of His existence. But beyond that, He promised, "I will come to you" (v. 18). Some say that this was a promise of the rapture. But if the verse refers to the rapture, it would say, "I will come *for* you." Others say it is only a promise that they would see Him after the resurrection. I do not think that is the best interpretation either, because He was on earth for only forty days after He rose. Such a short period seems like a small commodity of comfort.

What He seems rather to be speaking of is His spiritual presence

in every believer through the agency of the Holy Spirit. He was saying, "When the Spirit of God comes to reside in your life, I will be
there as well." In Matthew 28:20 He promises, "Lo, I am with you
always, even to the end of the age."

That is the mystery of the Trinity: the Holy Spirit abides in us (v.
17), Christ indwells us (Colossians 1:27), and God is in us (1 John
4:12). This presence is the source of eternal life. Jesus goes on to
say, "Because I live, you shall live also" (v. 19).

How is it that a man can sense the presence of God within Him?
How can he know the Spirit is there? He must be spiritually alive to
have spiritual perception. The spiritually dead man understands
nothing about God. He cannot respond to God.

But the person who is spiritually alive lives in another dimension.
He is alive to the spiritual world. And the basis of his life is the resurrection of Jesus Christ: "Because I live, you shall live also" (v. 19).
Eternal life is not the quantity of life; it is the kind of life that makes
you eternally sensitive to what God is doing. Here is the essence of
spiritual life: to be alive spiritually, walking with God, sensing the
Holy Spirit, communing with Christ, and moving and participating
in the spiritual realm. The world cannot know anything about that.

FULL UNDERSTANDING

Those who love Christ are not only indwelt by the Holy Spirit,
Christ, and the Father, but the believer enjoys a supernatural union
with them as well. Jesus illustrates this union by comparing it with
His relationship to the Father: "In that day you shall know that I
am in My Father, and you in Me, and I in you" (v. 20). We are one
with God and Christ. That is why sin is so out of place in the believer's life.

It is confusing to try to understand how we can be in Christ and
He in us. How can both things be true at once? It doesn't seem logical, but it is not supposed to be. We are so closely united spiritually
with Christ that the distinctions are difficult to sort out.

At this point, the disciples still did not understand the mystery of
the relation of the Son to the Father. Union with deity was such a
foreign concept to them that their minds could not conceive of it.
So Jesus said, "In that day you shall know" (v. 20). It seems clear
that He was referring to the day of Pentecost, on which the Holy
Spirit came. Before He came to dwell within them and teach them
the truth, they had no way of understanding the relation of God
and Christ and how it corresponded to their relationship with Him.

But as suddenly as they received the Holy Spirit in Acts 2, they began to understand. Peter was probably the best evidence of that. Bumbling, denying Peter, who rarely seemed to understand anything, stood up on the very day that the Spirit of God came to dwell within him and preached a powerful sermon, clearly delineating exactly who Jesus Christ is, who the Father is, how they are related, why Jesus came, why He died, why He rose, and what it all meant in reference to Israel.

Peter had not secretly acquired a seminary education or read all the good theology books. Those things were not even available. The Spirit of God had supernaturally untangled Peter's understanding, and everything had fallen into place for him. On that day he finally understood. It may not have made any more sense logically than it did before, but in a spiritual sense, he understood.

The Manifestation of the Father

In a beautiful summary, crushing the full bloom of redemption into one little wisp of fragrance, Jesus reviewed how a man comes into that supernatural union with Him: "He who has My commandments and keeps them, he it is who loves Me; and he who loves Me shall be loved by My Father, and I will love him, and will disclose Myself to him" (v. 21). He has come full circle to the point where He began in verse 15.

The Father wants to glorify the Son, and He continually does so. Anybody who loves the Son is thus loved of the Father. That is not difficult to understand from a human perspective. I find that I like people who like my children. How much more must God, whose love is perfect, love those who love His Son?

Not only that, but Jesus also promises to love them and to disclose Himself and the Father to them. That supernatural union comes with loving Jesus Christ, a personal love relationship between the believer and Christ — not religion, cranking out the motions, going to church and going through some kind of ritual — but an honest, deep, heartfelt, committed kind of love that obeys. To that kind of love comes the manifestation of God in all His fullness and the union that results.

I am sure all the disciples were dumbfounded at that point. Judas — not Judas Iscariot but the disciple who is also called Lebbaeus and Thaddaeus — spoke out: "Lord, what then has happened that You are going to disclose Yourself to us, and not to the world?" (v. 22). He thought Jesus meant that He would physically manifest Himself and the Father. Yet he reasoned that if they could see Jesus, everyone else should be able to as well. Furthermore, Christ was to be the Savior of the world. How could He not manifest Himself to the world?

"Jesus answered and said to him, 'If anyone loves Me, he will keep My word; and My Father will love him, and We will come to him, and make Our abode with him. He who does not love Me does not keep My words; and the word which you hear is not Mine, but the Father's who sent Me' " (vv. 23-24). Thaddaeus might not have been much satisfied with that answer; it sounds exactly like verse 21, which sounds exactly like verse 15. They all say the same thing: "If you love Me, you will keep My commandments, and I will manifest Myself to you."

The point Jesus is making to Thaddaeus — and it is an important concept — is that He is talking about manifesting Himself in a spiritual sense — revealing Himself and the Father in a man's heart, to his spiritual senses. An unsaved man does not have spiritual perception; the only one who can comprehend the manifestation Christ is talking about is one who loves Him and shows his love by obedience.

It is not a question of perfection — if we say we are without sin, we call God a liar (cf. 1 John 1:10). Nor is the issue one of earning salvation with obedience. Salvation is a gift that comes by faith. It cannot be earned or deserved. But faith that does not produce obedience is not saving faith (see James 2:17). The issue is not perfection but the direction of the redeemed life. The Lord has fellowship only with those whose hearts welcome Him and love Him and whose love is clearly indicated by their obedience. They are the ones who are truly redeemed. The world will never discern Jesus Christ because the world will not love Him. The world will never discern the Father because the Father reveals Himself only to those who love the Son.

Jesus continues: "He who does not love Me does not keep My words; and the word which you hear is not Mine, but the Father's who sent Me" (v. 24). How can He manifest Himself to someone who is disobedient? The world does not want Christ. It does not want to obey His words. It does not love Him. And since the words Jesus spoke came from the Father, the world does not want Him either. Jesus Christ manifests Himself only to those who want Him. There is not a soul in the world who wants Jesus Christ to the point of loving obedience who does not receive Him. The reason the world does not receive the manifestation of God is that those in the world do not want Him. And He will not manifest Himself to an unbelieving, unwanting, unloving world.

Note that Jesus claimed His words are the Father's. It was the highest claim to authority He could make. He was in essence saying, "If you reject My words, you have rejected God." His words are the Father's truth. Christ had subjugated His own thoughts, words, ideas, and attitudes to the will of the Father, so that though the Father and the Son were always in perfect harmony, nevertheless, the Son was totally yielded to the Father's will. In other words, when Jesus said, "Not My will, but Thine" (Luke 22:42), He was implying that their wills were different. The Son did all that He did, not because it was *His* will, but because it was the *Father's*.

A Supernatural Teacher

Jesus had spoken only the Father's words, but the disciples had always had trouble understanding. For example, in John 2:22 we read, "When therefore He was raised from the dead, His disciples remembered that He said this; and they believed the Scripture, and the word which Jesus had spoken." John 12:16 says, "These things His disciples did not understand at the first; but when Jesus was glorified, then they remembered that these things were written of Him, and that they had done these things to Him." In John 16:12, Jesus says, "I have many more things to say to you, but you cannot bear them now." They had failed to understand so much of what He had already said, that He had to call a halt to it.

Now He was turning over the continuing teaching to the Holy Spirit, who would dwell in them. "These things I have spoken to you, while abiding with you. But the Helper, the Holy Spirit, whom the Father will send in My name, He will teach you all things, and bring to your remembrance all that I said to you" (vv. 25-26). All these three years He had been telling them the Father's truth. But they never really understood much. Now He would send them a resident Teacher to dwell within.

The Holy Spirit comes in the name of Christ. That means, of course, that He comes in Christ's stead. Christ had come in the name of the Father. Neither carries on His own ministry independently. The Holy Spirit's ministry is to stand in this world in the place of Christ. He desires what Christ desires, loves what Christ loves, does what Christ would do, and thus brings glory to Christ, not to Himself.

Therefore, God gave His truth to Christ, who gave it to the Holy Spirit, who reveals it to us. The Spirit receives nothing of Himself, seeks no glory of His own, and desires only to manifest the glory of Jesus Christ.

His role is that of a Teacher: "He will teach you all things, and bring to your remembrance all that I said to you" (v. 26). That does not mean, of course, that the Holy Spirit imparts to us some kind of omniscience. "All things" is used here in a relative sense. It means "all things pertaining to spiritual maturity."

A secondary application of this promise is that the Holy Spirit would enable those disciples to recall the words Jesus had spoken to them so that when they recorded them as Scripture, they would be perfect and error free. It was a promise of divine inspiration.

Can you imagine their trying, without supernatural help, to put together a record of Jesus' words? They had to have a supernatural Teacher to record accurately Jesus' words as Scripture. In addition, the Spirit would reveal new truth. Those whom God chose wrote it down, resulting in the Word of God as we have it today. To question the accuracy or the integrity of it is to deny this crucial aspect of the Spirit's role.

Faith in the inerrancy of biblical inspiration is fundamental to sound doctrine. Those who give up the inspiration of the Bible have given up the basis of Christianity. History has repeatedly borne that out. Churches, seminaries, and denominations that have yielded ground on the issue of inspiration have opened the floodgates to rationalism, to compromise, and, ultimately, to total apostasy.

How does the promise that the Holy Spirit will instruct us and bring all things to our memory apply today? The Spirit guides us in our pursuit of truth through the Word of God. He teaches us by convicting us of sin, affirming the truth in our hearts, and opening our understanding to the depth of truth God has revealed. He often brings to mind appropriate verses and truths from Scripture at just the right time.

Matthew 10:19 is a promise given to the apostles as Christ sent them on a mission to preach among the cities, but it shows how the Spirit of God works, even today: "But when they deliver you up [to be tried for your faith], do not become anxious about how or what you will speak; for it shall be given you in that hour what you are to speak."

Nothing can take the place of the Holy Spirit's work in the life of the believer. Through Him we are "heirs of God and fellow heirs with Christ" (Romans 8:17). We are infinitely richer than all the millionaires of the world put together, because what we possess is not a passing thing — ours is an eternal inheritance.

Paul, quoting Isaiah, writes, "Things which eye has not seen and ear has not heard, and which have not entered the heart of man, all that God has prepared for those who love him" (1 Corinthians 2:9). Christians are rich beyond imagination. And the greatest resource of all — the Holy Spirit — dwells in us and is with us forever.

7

The Gift of Peace

The Hebrew Bible uses a familiar but significant word, *shalom*. In its purest sense, *shalom* means "peace." The connotation is positive. That is, when someone says, *"Shalom,"* or, "Peace unto you," he does not mean, "I hope you don't get into any trouble"; he means, "I hope you have the highest good coming your way."

Most people in our world do not understand peace as a positive concept. All they know is the negative aspect of peace, which is merely the absence of trouble. The definition of *peace* in many languages of the world illustrates that. For example, the Quechua Indians in Equador and Bolivia use a word for peace that literally translates "to sit down in one's heart." For them, peace is the opposite of running around in the midst of constant anxieties. The Chol Indians of Mexico define peace as "a quiet heart." These may be beautiful ways to put it, but they still leave us with only the negative idea that peace is the absence of trouble.

Closer to the meaning of the Hebrew word *shalom* is the word used by the Kekchi Indians of Guatemala, who define peace as "quiet goodness." The term they use conveys the idea of something that is active and aggressive, not just a rest in one's own heart away from troublesome circumstances.

The biblical concept of peace does not focus on the absence of trouble. Biblical peace is unrelated to circumstances; it is a goodness of life that is not touched by what happens on the outside. You may be in the midst of great trials and still have biblical peace. Paul said he could be content in any circumstance; and he demonstrated that he had peace even in the jail at Philippi, where he sang and remained confident that God was being gracious to him. Then when the opportunity arose, he communicated God's goodness to the Philippian jailer and brought him and his family to salvation. Likewise, James wrote, "Consider it all joy, my brethren, when you encounter various trials" (James 1:2).

Where does a man find the kind of peace that is not just the absence of trouble — the kind of peace that cannot be affected by problems, danger, or sorrow? It is ironic that what is surely the most definitive discourse on peace in all of Scripture comes from the Lord Jesus on the night before He died in agony. He knew what He was facing, yet He still took time to comfort His disciples with the message of peace:

> Peace I leave with you; My peace I give to you; not as the world gives, do I give to you. Let not your heart be troubled, nor let it be fearful.
>
> (John 14:27)

The peace Jesus was speaking of enables believers to remain calm in the most wildly fearful circumstances. It enables them to hush a cry, still a riot, rejoice in pain and trial, and sing in the middle of suffering. This peace is never affected by circumstances but instead affects and even overrules them.

THE NATURE OF PEACE

The New Testament speaks of two kinds of peace — the objective peace that has to do with your relation to God and the subjective peace that has to do with your experience in life.

The natural man lacks peace with God. We all come into the world fighting against God, because we are a part of the rebellion that started with Adam and Eve. Romans 5:10 says that we were enemies of God. We fought against God, and everything we did militated against His principles.

But when we receive Jesus Christ, we cease being enemies of God — we make a truce with Him. We come over to His side, and the hostility is ended. Jesus Christ wrote the treaty with the blood of His cross. That treaty, that bond, that covenant of peace declares the objective fact that we now are at peace with Him.

That is what Paul means in Ephesians 6:15, where he calls the good news of salvation "The preparation of the gospel of peace." The gospel is that which makes a man who was at war with God to be at peace with Him. This peace is objective — it has nothing to do with how we feel or what we think. It is an accomplished fact.

Romans 5:1 says, "Therefore having been justified by faith, we have peace with God." We who trust Christ are redeemed and declared righteous by faith. Our sins are forgiven, rebellion has ceased, the war is over, and we have peace with God. That was God's wonderful purpose in salvation.

Colossians 1:20-22 says that Christ "made peace through the blood of His cross. . . . And although you were formerly alienated and hostile in mind, engaged in evil deeds, yet He has now reconciled you in His fleshly body through death, in order to present you before Him holy and blameless and beyond reproach."

A sinful, vile, wicked man cannot come into the presence of a holy God. Something must make that unholy man righteous before he can be at peace with God. And that is exactly what Christ did, dying for sin, imputing His righteousness to man. So Paul says we are no longer enemies but are at peace because we are reconciled.

It is as if God were on one side, we were on the other side, and Christ then filled the gap, taking the hand of God and the hand of man and placing them together in the same grip. We have been brought together through the blood of the cross of Jesus Christ. Whereas God and man were once estranged, they have now been reconciled. That is the heart of the gospel message, as Paul says in 2 Corinthians 5:18-19.

But Jesus is not talking about objective peace in verse 27. The peace He speaks of in that verse is a subjective, experiential peace. It is tranquility of soul, a settled, positive peace that affects the circumstances of life. It is peace that is aggressive. Rather than being victimized by events, it attacks them and gobbles them up. It is a supernatural, permanent, positive, no-side-effects, divine tranquilizer. This peace is the heart's calm after Calvary's storm. It is the firm conviction that He who spared not His own Son will also along with Him freely give us all things (cf. Romans 8:32).

This is the peace that Paul speaks about in Philippians 4:7: "And the peace of God, which surpasses all comprehension, shall guard your hearts and your minds in Christ Jesus." Unlike the world's peace, the peace of God is not based on circumstances, so it does not always make sense to the carnal mind. Paul says it is a peace that surpasses comprehension. It does not seem reasonable that such peace could exist in the midst of the problems and troubles Christians go through. But this is divine, supernatural peace; it cannot be figured out on a human level.

The Greek word for *guard* in Philippians 4:7 is not the word that means "watch" or "keep imprisoned." It is a word that is often used in a military sense, meaning "to stand at a post and guard against the aggression of an enemy." When peace is on guard, the Christian has entered an impregnable citadel from which nothing can dislodge him. The name of the fortress is Christ, and the guard is peace. The peace of God stands guard and keeps worry from corroding our hearts and unworthy thoughts from tearing up our minds.

That is the kind of peace men truly want. They want a peace that deals with the past, one where they are not tortured hour by hour by the poison of past sins. They want a peace that governs the present and does not allow unsatisfied desires to gnaw at their hearts. They want a peace that holds promise for the future, a peace in which there are no forboding fears of the unknown or threats of a dark tomorrow. And that is exactly the peace that Jesus left with His disciples. It is a peace through which the guilt of the past is forgiven, by which the trials of the present are overcome, and in which our destiny in the future is secured eternally.

THE SOURCE OF PEACE

That subjective, experiential peace — the peace *of* God — has its foundation in the objective, factual peace — peace *with* God. The peace of God is not obtainable by those who are not at peace with God. God alone brings peace. In fact, in Philippians 4:9, 1 Thessalonians 5:23, and again in Hebrews 13:20, He is called "the God of peace."

Jesus Christ is also seen as the One who gives peace. Jesus said, "My peace I give to you." Notice He says "*My* peace." Here is the key to the supernaturalness of this peace — it is His own personal peace. It is the same deep, rich peace that stilled His heart in the midst of mockers, haters, murderers, traitors, and everything else He faced. He had a calm about Him that was unnatural and superhuman. In the midst of incomprehensible resistance and persecution, He was calm and unfaltering; He was a rock.

Those who knew Him might have come to expect it, but you can imagine how it must have confounded His enemies and those who did not know Him to see someone that calm. When Jesus appeared before Pilate, He was so calm, so serene, so controlled, and so at peace that Pilate became greatly disturbed. He was furious that Jesus was standing before him, fearless; and in a near frenzy, Pilate said, "Do You not know that I have authority to release You, and I have authority to crucify You?" (John 19:10).

Then in perfect peace Jesus replied, "You would have no authority over Me, unless it had been given you from above" (John 19:11). That is the kind of peace Jesus is talking about in verse 27. That is the kind He gives to us. It is undistracted fearlessness and trust. So the source of peace is Christ.

In fact, Christ is seen throughout the New Testament as the dispenser of peace. In Acts 10:36, Peter says, "The word which He sent to the sons of Israel, preaching peace through Jesus Christ." Second Thessalonians 3:16 says, "Now may the Lord of peace Himself continually grant you peace." Jesus Christ gives us His own personal peace. It has been tested — it was His own shield and His own helmet that served Him in battle. And He gave it to us when He left. It should give us the same serenity in danger, the same calm in trouble, and the same freedom from anxiety.

THE GIVER OF PEACE

The Holy Spirit is the giver of this peace, and He dispenses it as a gift. Galatians 5:22 says that one aspect of the fruit of the Spirit is peace. You might ask: If it was Christ's peace, why is the Holy Spirit giving it? The answer is in John 16:14, which says, "He shall glorify Me; for He shall take of Mine, and shall disclose it to you." The Holy Spirit's ministry is to take the things of Christ and give them to us.

Notice that every promise Jesus made to His troubled disciples on the night before His death was rooted in the coming of the Holy Spirit. Christ promised life, union with deity, full understanding, and peace to those who are His disciples, but it is the Spirit of God who takes the things of Christ and gives them to us.

THE CONTRAST OF PEACE

In verse 27, Jesus says, "Not as the world gives, do I give to you." In other words, His peace is not like the peace of the world. The world's peace is worthless. *The New York Times* observed that the world has had more than 50 wars in the last seventeen years. At least 21 of those wars have been large scale. Since 36 B.C., there have been 14,553 wars. Before World War II, the world had an average of 2.61 new wars every year. But since World War II, despite mankind's so-called enlightenment and despite all of the organized efforts for world peace, there have been on the average 3 new wars every year. The *Times* closed the article by saying, "Peace is a fable."

Man does not know peace. He is not even at peace in his own house. Homes are shattered and torn apart. There is no communication, no love, no care, and no concern. There is no peace in the heart, no peace in the family, no peace in our schools, no peace on the job, no peace in the nation, and certainly no peace in the world.

The only peace this world can know is shallow and unfulfilling. For most persons, the pursuit of peace is only an attempt to get away from problems. That is why people seek peace through alcohol, drugs, or other forms of escapism. The fact is, apart from God, there is no real peace in this world. The peace of putting your blinders on, of going to bed and forgetting it, is fleeting and worthless. And yet men try desperately to hold onto this kind of mock peace.

It is a futile pursuit. Godless men can never know true peace. They might know only a momentary tranquility — a shallow feeling, perhaps stimulated by positive circumstances mixed with a great deal of ignorance. In fact, if unsaved men knew what destiny awaited them without God, the illusory peace borne out of ignorance would evaporate instantly.

Men today live in a form of existential shock. They do not understand their own being, and they do not know who they are, where they are going, or what they are going to do when they get there — if they get there. I recently saw a sign on a man's desk that said, "I've got so many troubles that if anything else happens to me, it will be two weeks before I can even worry about it."

That is a commentary on the plight of modern man, but the truth is, the real reason a person cannot find peace has nothing to do with emotions or environment. If you lack peace, it is not because of your mother, your father, your grandmother, the church you were raised in, or a bad experience you had when you were a child. The Bible tells us why men do not know peace. Jeremiah 17:9 says, "The heart is more deceitful than all else and is desperately sick." The King James Version reads, "desperately wicked." Isaiah 48:22 says, " 'There is no peace for the wicked,' says the Lord." Man's heart is desperately wicked, and thus he cannot find peace.

Throughout the land of Judah in Jeremiah's day problems were rising up fast. A great army was coming to destroy Jerusalem and take the people into captivity, and they were frightened. Peace was being removed from the land, and there was destruction coming such as they had never experienced.

Jeremiah 6:14 says, "They have healed the brokenness of My people superficially, saying, 'Peace, peace,' but there is no peace." In other words, they had tried to patch up their evil ways, saying, "Peace, peace, everything is OK." There was a great deal of talk about peace, but there was no genuine peace. In chapter 8 of Jeremiah, the prophet says, "We waited for peace, but no good came; for a time of healing, but behold, terror!" (v. 15).

A few chapters later, the prophet repeats the observation: "Hast Thou completely rejected Judah? Or hast thou loathed Zion? Why hast Thou stricken us so that we are beyond healing? We waited for peace, but nothing good came; and for a time of healing, but behold, terror!" (v. 19). Then Jeremiah put his finger on the source of the trouble: " 'Do not enter a house of mourning, or go to lament or to console them; for I have withdrawn My peace from this people,' declares the Lord" (16:5). Where there was sin, there could be no peace.

We can expect nothing different in the end times. Revelation 6:4 says that during the Tribulation there will be a brief period of peace, but after about three and a half years, peace will be taken from the earth. Luke 21:26 says that men's hearts will fail them for fear. In other words, people will be dropping dead from heart attacks motivated by fear.

The world's peace does not exist. It is a lie and cannot exist. No man without Jesus Christ can ever have peace, and no world without God can ever know peace. If a man has a moment of peace in this world, it is only a camouflage hiding the eternal pressure of God's judgment.

THE RESULT OF PEACE

Jesus shows us the proper response to His promise of peace: "Let not your heart be troubled, nor let it be fearful" (v. 27). We ought to be able to lay hold of this peace. It is there, it is ours; but we must take hold of it. It is interesting that He says, "I give you peace," and then says, "Let not your heart be troubled." The peace He gives has to be received and applied in our lives. If we lay hold of the promise of the very peace of Christ, we *will* have calm, untroubled hearts regardless of external circumstances.

If you have a troubled heart, it is because you do not believe God — you do not genuinely trust His promise of peace. Anxiety and turmoil seldom focus on present circumstances. Normally, anxiety is trouble borrowed from either the past or the future. Some people worry about things that *might* happen. The anxieties of others come out of the past. But both the future and the past are under the care of God. He promises to supply our future need, and He has forgiven the past. Do not worry about tomorrow or yesterday. Jesus said, "Each day has enough trouble of its own" (Matthew 6:34). Concentrate on trusting God for today's needs.

The peace of Christ is a great resource in helping us to know the will of God. Colossians 3:15 says, "And let the peace of Christ rule in your hearts, to which indeed you were called in one body; and be thankful." The word translated "rule" is the Greek word *brabeuo*, which means "umpire." Paul is urging the Colossians to so depend on the peace of Christ that it becomes an umpire in the decisions they have to make in life.

Do you have a problem, or a decision to make? Let the peace of Christ make that decision for you. If you have examined a planned action in the light of God's Word, and God's Word does not forbid you from going ahead with it, then if you can do it and retain the peace of Christ in your heart, do it with the confidence that it is God's will. But if you find you do not have a sense of peace and God's blessing, do not do it.

Don't try to rationalize about it. You may find it makes good sense from the rational point of view. But will it rob your soul of rest and peace? Do you have a sense of confidence that God is in it? If you do not have peace, it is probably the wrong thing to do. Let Christ's peace be the umpire that makes the calls. That is how we are to govern our behavior.

There are two conspicuous reasons I do not like to sin. One is that sin is an offense to the holy God I love. He hates sin, and my love for Him makes me want to please Him. The other reason is that I do not like the way I feel after I sin. Sin destroys my sense of peace, and it breaks my sense of communion with God.

Look again at Colossians 3:15. Paul says there that peace belongs to every Christian. He calls it "the peace of Christ . . . to which indeed you were called in one body." Our peace with God and the peace of God that rules our hearts is a foundation of Christian unity. If we disregard that peace, if we refuse to let it be the umpire, we cannot have unity in the Body of Christ, for everyone will be doing his own thing, and the Body will be divided.

The peace of Christ is also an unending source of strength in the midst of difficulties. As Stephen sank bleeding and bruised under the stones of a cursing mob, he offered a loving, forgiving prayer for his murderers: "Lord, do not hold this sin against them!" (Acts 7:60). Paul was driven out of one city, dragged almost lifeless out of another, stripped by robbers, and arraigned before ruler after ruler. Yet he had an uncanny peace. He wrote:

> Five times I received from the Jews thirty-nine lashes. Three times I was beaten with rods, once I was stoned, three times I was shipwrecked, a night and a day I have spent in the deep. I have

been on frequent journeys, in dangers from rivers, dangers from robbers, dangers from my countrymen, dangers from the Gentiles, dangers in the city, dangers in the wilderness, dangers on the sea, dangers among false brethren; I have been in labor and hardship, through many sleepless nights, in hunger and thirst, often without food, in cold and exposure. Apart from such external things, there is the daily pressure upon me of concern for all the churches. Who is weak without my being weak? Who is led into sin without my intense concern?

(2 Corinthians 11:24-29)

That is the same peace you and I have; Paul just applied it. He said:

We are afflicted in every way, but not crushed; perplexed, but not despairing; persecuted, but not forsaken; struck down, but not destroyed; always carrying about in the body the dying of Jesus, that the life of Jesus also may be manifested in our body. For we who live are constantly being delivered over to death for Jesus' sake, that the life of Jesus also may be manifested in our mortal flesh.

(2 Corinthians 4:8-11)

But he wrote several verses later: "Therefore we do not lose heart, but though our outer man is decaying, yet our inner man is being renewed day by day. For momentary, light affliction is producing for us an eternal weight of glory far beyond all comparison, while we look not at the things which are seen, but at the things which are not seen; for the things which are seen are temporal, but the things which are not seen are eternal" (vv. 16-18). In other words, Paul did not focus on his problems but instead on the promises of God to sustain and ultimately to glorify him. Trouble comes and goes, but glory is eternal. Paul understood that, and that is why in the midst of his trials he could write to the Philippians, "Rejoice in the Lord always; again I will say, rejoice!" (Philippians 4:4).

To have that supernatural peace available puts us under obligation to lean on it. Colossians 3:15 is not a command to seek peace but rather a plea to let the Lord's peace work in us: "And let the peace of Christ rule in your hearts." You have this peace; now let it rule.

Perfect peace comes when our focus is off the problem, off the trouble, and constantly on Christ. Isaiah 26:3 says, "The steadfast of mind Thou wilt keep in perfect peace, because he trusts in Thee."

In the midst of a society where we are constantly bombarded with advertising and other wordly pressures designed to get us to focus on our needs and problems, how can we keep our minds focused on Christ? By studying the Word of God and being taught by the Holy Spirit and by permitting Him to fix our hearts on the person of Jesus Christ.

Most people who lack peace simply have not taken the time to pursue it. God's peace comes to those with the personal discipline to stop in the midst of the maelstrom of life and take time to seek Him. It is a condition of peace that we cease from life's activity and know Him. He commands, "Be still, and know that I am God" (Psalm 46:10, KJV). And to those whose minds are steadfastly fixed on Him, He gives the gift of peace.

8

What Jesus' Death Meant to Him

As we look back on the cross after almost two thousand years, we stand in awe at all that was accomplished there for us. There the very Son of God suffered shame and ridicule at the hands of wicked, murdering men. He did it willingly to provide forgiveness for our sins and access to God. God's judgment was stayed, and the righteousness of Christ became ours. He set us free to commune with Him, and we became His children.

Jn 16: 27

When the disciples looked forward to the cross, they could only wonder what it meant. They had been with Jesus for three blessed years, during which He had loved them and supplied all their needs. When they heard Him talk about His death, they found it impossible to understand. How could God incarnate die, and what would life be like without their beloved Master and Teacher? Fear must have come over them at the mere thought of it; and then when they realized the time was at hand, the anticipation of loneliness set in. Looking ahead at it that awful night before He died, they could see nothing but the oppressive specter of tragedy.

The problem was their perspective. They were looking at His death from their own viewpont — they gave little thought to what it meant to Him. Their faith was weak, but beyond that they had a simple problem: selfishness. Because He loved them and took care of them, they wanted Jesus to stay with them. In a sense they were acting like the multitudes who followed Jesus as long as He fed them but did not want to pay the price of following Him whole-heartedly. The disciples were moping around, brooding, stewing over their own dilemma, thinking only of how Jesus' death would affect *their* problems and *their* desires. Their love was superficial and based on a desire for their own good, not on a desire for the best welfare of the One they loved.

We tend to respond that way when death touches us. We feel great sorrow but often for the wrong reasons. We may wonder why God would take *our* loved one — as if we should have some guaranteed amount of time here together. When a Christian dies, sorrow is normal for a while, and tears can be healthy, but when mourning continues for a long time, it may be because the grieving person is seeing the death only from his own perspective of personal loss instead of from the loved one's point of view of eternal glory. We must see death from the right perspective — as ultimate release from the body of sin and unending joy in heaven.

Jesus' death, however, was not release from a body of sin but rather was the ravaging of a sinless body through the bearing of the sins of the world. And before He could enter into unending joy, our Lord would face a dreadful, eternal moment of separation from the Father and the force of all mankind's deserved punishment.

Nevertheless, He anticipated it all with an eager heart. As the cross drew near, He revealed to His disciples what it meant to Him:

> You heard that I said to you, "I go away, and I will come to you." If you loved Me, you would have rejoiced, because I go to the Father; for the Father is greater than I. And now I have told you before it comes to pass, that when it comes to pass, you may believe. I will not speak much more with you, for the ruler of the world is coming, and he has nothing in Me; but that the world may know that I love the Father, and as the Father gave Me commandment, even so I do. Arise, let us go from here.
>
> (John 14:28-31)

The disciples viewed it with sorrow, but to Him it meant joy. Had they loved Him, they would have rejoiced with Him and looked forward with Him to the four marvelous eternal works that would be accomplished at the cross.

HIS PERSON WOULD BE DIGNIFIED

Before the incarnation, Jesus was in eternal glory. He experienced the Father's infinite love and fellowship in a way we cannot comprehend. But He left this glory to come to earth, not as a king to a magnificent palace but as a tiny baby to a stinking stable. He lived in poverty. He had no place even to lay His head. He suffered the hatred, abuse, and jeers of evil men. He was rejected by His own people and vilified even by the religious leaders. "He was despised and forsaken of men, a man of sorrows, and acquainted with grief; and like one from whom men hide their face" (Isaiah 53:3).

From our human perspective, one of the most incomprehensive truths about Jesus Christ is that He, the eternal Lord of Glory, was willing to humble Himself like that for our sakes. He stepped down from a position of equality with the Most High God and condescended to share His riches with us. Second Corinthians 8:9 says, "For you know the grace of our Lord Jesus Christ, that though He was rich, yet for your sake He became poor, that you through His poverty might become rich." Jesus had all the riches of heaven, yet He gave them up for a while so that we could share them with Him forever.

The book of Hebrews also tells us about Jesus' condescension:

> But we do see Him who has been made for a little while lower than the angels . . . because of the suffering of death crowned with glory and honor, that by the grace of God He might taste death for everyone. . . . Therefore, He had to be made like His brethren in all things, that He might become a merciful and faithful high priest in things pertaining to God, to make propitiation for the sins of the people. For since He Himself was tempted in that which He has suffered, he is able to come to the aid of those who are tempted.
>
> (Hebrews 2:9, 17-18)

Jesus became one of us. He suffered what we suffer, not only so that He could redeem us but also so that He could sympathize with us. The incarnation allowed Him to experience all the temptations, difficulties, griefs, and heartbreaks of people. He can empathize with us, and He can understand our struggles from His own experience.

Philippians 2 describes the incarnation as an act of unselfish humility on the part of Jesus, "who, although He existed in the form of God, did not regard equality with God a thing to be grasped" (v. 6). He was equal to God but did not covet the outward appearance of equality. Instead, He "emptied Himself, taking the form of a bond-servant, and being made in the likeness of men. And being found in appearance as a man, He humbled Himself by becoming obedient to the point of death, even death on a cross" (vv. 7-8). He was willing to come down to earth and become a servant, even if it meant death on a cross.

Because He humbly obeyed, God exalted Him. Paul continues, "Therefore also God highly exalted Him, and bestowed on Him the name which is above every name, that at the name of Jesus every knee should bow, of those who are in heaven, and on earth, and under the earth" (vv. 9-10).

There have always been those who are confused about the humiliation of Christ. They think that because He humbled Himself and became a servant, they are not to worship Him as God. Actually, the opposite is true. Because He humbled Himself He is to be exalted; every knee is to bow before Him and confess that Jesus Christ is Lord.

Jehovah's Witnesses, Unitarians, and others who deny the deity of Christ have misinterpreted verse 28 by saying that Jesus is inferior to the Father. They refuse to grasp that when He said, "The Father is greater than I," He referred not to His essential being, but to His role as a humbled servant. During the period Jesus was humbled, the Father was in glory and therefore greater; Jesus had put Himself beneath the Father's glory.

He had also put His will beneath the Father's will. In the Garden of Gethsemane, He prayed to the Father, "Remove this cup from Me; yet not what I will, but what Thou wilt" (Mark 14:36).

Jesus repeatedly claimed to be equal in deity to the Father. Just one example is in verse 9, where Philip asks to be shown the Father. Jesus answers, "He who has seen Me has seen the Father." Jesus took on a *role* that was beneath the Father, but He was not inferior in nature or essence (cf. Titus 2:13).

At the end of His earthly ministry, as He approached the cross, knowing what lay ahead of Him, Christ knelt in the Garden of Gethsemane and prayed to the Father: "I glorified Thee on the earth, having accomplished the work which Thou has given Me to do. And now, glorify Thou Me together with Thyself, Father, with the glory which I had with Thee before the world was" (John 17:4-5). He was looking ahead to the full expression of His glory — that same pristine glory He knew before the humiliation of the incarnation.

The hatred and abuse were almost over. Death would end them, and He would return to the glory He once had with the Father. He found joy as He approached the cross, because through His suffering there He would be restored to the full expression of deity. He looked forward to it. He rejoiced in anticipation of it. And He wanted His beloved friends to share His joy. "If you loved Me," He told them, "you would have rejoiced, because I go to the Father; for the Father is greater than I" (v. 28).

Hebrews 12:2 says, "[Jesus,] for the joy set before Him endured the cross, despising the shame, and has sat down at the right hand of the throne of God." He rejoiced because He knew the result of the cross would be His glorification, and He knew He would soon be with the Father at His right hand.

Some people think Jesus did not know that He was going to be crucified. He knew. He was familiar with the prophecies of Isaiah 53 and Psalm 22, both of which contain detailed accounts of the crucifixion. They were written long before Christ's birth, and, obviously, He knew them. The crucifixion was not an afterthought but a crucial element in the plan of God from the beginning. Our Lord knew exactly what was going to happen, but He went to the cross anyway. It was a bitter cup, but He was willing to drink it.

THE TRUTH WOULD BE DOCUMENTED

Jesus made many claims about Himself to the disciples. Although they wanted to believe those claims — and for the most part they did believe them — yet doubt often crept into their hearts. They found much of Jesus' teaching about who He was and why He came difficult to fathom, so they teetered between belief and unbelief.

Jesus used a simple method to strengthen their faith — He predicted events. When what He said happened, the disciples remembered what He had said. One prophecy after another came true, and each one grounded their faith a little more. By the day of Pentecost, their faith was so strong that they fearlessly set off the explosion of Christianity all over the world.

In verse 29, Jesus acknowledged this method of strengthening them: "I have told you before it comes to pass, that when it comes to pass, you may believe." He knew that they did not believe everything then, but that they would believe when His words came true.

Fulfilled prophecy is perhaps the greatest proof that the Word of God is true. It carries the weight of proof for the Word of God further than any other single element of Scripture.

Not too long ago I was talking to a man who said that Israel no longer has a place in the plan of God. I pointed out to him that Scripture prophesied that Israel would be regathered in the land — just the way we see it happening today. Then I asked him, "What does your theology do with that?" He replied, "It wiggles a lot." Fulfilled prophecy has a devastating way of dealing with human doubt.

In John 13:19, Jesus has used the same method to strengthen the disciples' faith. There is a deep significance in His words at the end of verse 19: "That . . . you may believe that I am He." Notice that the "He" at the end of the verse was added by the English translators. What Jesus actually said was, "I am telling you before, so that you will believe that I am." "I AM" is God's name (Exodus 3:14). It was the same as saying, "I want you to believe that I am God." He was urging them to embrace the truth of His deity.

He had just told them, among other things, that Judas was going to betray Him. You can imagine what the disciples thought later when they saw Judas betray Jesus in the garden. Their minds must have flashed back to what He had said earlier in the upper room. He had given a string of prophecies that began with the betrayal by Judas and ended with the promise of a divine Helper. Their faith was solid by the time the last prediction was fulfilled on the day of Pentecost.

That final promise of a divine Helper was linked with a promise of supernatural peace. On the day of Pentecost, a supernatural peace like nothing they had ever known flooded their hearts as the Spirit of God took residence within them. Later, when Peter and John preached, the religious authorities confronted them and ordered them to stop. They calmly responded, "Whether it is right in the sight of God to give heed to you rather than to God, you be the judge; for we cannot stop speaking what we have seen and heard" (Acts 4:19-20).

One by one, every prophecy He had given them had come to pass. With each one, their faith was strengthened so that they trusted more and more. The fulfilled prophecies fully documented the truth that He was God.

You may wonder why, if Jesus wanted to strengthen them, He did not simply stay on earth and continue teaching them. The reason was that He had said all He could say. Now it was time to leave so that other prophecies could come true. God's purpose in redemption could be fulfilled, and their faith could be strengthened as they watched it all unfold.

Their faith *was* strengthened by the events that followed. He had said He would die by being lifted up on a cross, and He did. He had said He would rise, and He did. He had said He would ascend to the Father, and they saw Him ascend. He had said the Spirit would come, and it happened. He had said He would supply supernatural life, and they got it. He had promised them a supernatural union with the living God, and they experienced it. He had promised them an indwelling Teacher, and they received the Spirit of God.

He had promised them peace, and they were flooded with peace. Every detail of each prophecy came to pass just as He had said. Through that, the disciples' faith became rock solid. His words were thus documented and their faith cemented.

His leaving was really an act of love for the disciples. He knew that their faith would have to be strong if they were to carry the message to the world. They would have to move into the full blast of Satan's fire, into the hotbed of the furnace. The only way their faith could remain strong enough was through seeing all His prophecies fulfilled one after another.

In fact, Jesus said that if they really loved him — if they really wanted the world to hear the gospel — they would rejoice that He was leaving. In effect he was saying, "Stop looking at My death from your own perspective and look at it from My perspective. When I go, your faith will be strengthened because the truth will be documented in your lives; then you will take My message into all the world. But the longer I stay, the longer that will be postponed."

HIS FOE WOULD BE DEFEATED

When Jesus came to earth, His central purpose was to redeem man. In Adam, man had fallen out of fellowship with God. Now man was separated from God and had neither communion with Him nor knowledge of Him. Christ had determined even before the foundation of the world that He would come to earth to bring fallen men back to God (cf. Revelation 13:8).

In order to succeed, He had to defeat Satan decisively. In verse 30, He talks about His foe. "I will not speak much more with you, for the ruler of the world is coming, and he has nothing in Me." He calls the devil "the ruler of the world" because this world is Satan's domain, and the system of evil under which this world is oppressed is of Satan's devising.

Satan was already indwelling Judas, pushing him into the garden, where he would betray Jesus. Jesus knew that Satan was coming in the person of Judas to take Him. He knew He was about to enter the dreaded death-battle with His enemy.

Jesus had battled Satan all through His earthly life. Satan tried to kill Him as an infant — he had caused all the male babies to be slain throughout the region where Jesus was born (Matthew 2:16). Although the Bible is largely silent regarding the first thirty years of Jesus' life, He undoubtedly faced satanic opposition at every turn. Then when He began His ministry, Satan immediately took Him out to the wilderness to tempt Him. He tried to get Jesus to bow and worship him. During Jesus' ministry, Satan tried everything. He confronted Him with people who hated Him and tried to kill Him, and with demons who tried to stop His work.

From the night of His birth to the night of His death, Satan fought Him. Finally, His death would resolve the age-old conflict that had raged since Lucifer's fall from heaven (cf. Isaiah 14 and Ezekiel 28). The outcome would be decided in this final conflict. He was about to win the ultimate victory.

He had looked forward to victory over Satan. Earlier, He had said, "Now judgment is upon this world; now the ruler of this world shall be cast out. And I, if I be lifted up from the earth, will draw all men to Myself." John adds an editorial note to those words: "But He was saying this to indicate the kind of death by which He was to die" (John 12:31-33). In other words, our Lord was saying that the ultimate defeat of Satan would be accomplished when He was "lifted up" on the cross. He went to the cross knowing it was the final blow that would wipe out Satan's power.

While Jesus was in the garden, the soldiers arrived. He asked them, "Have you come out with swords and clubs as against a robber? . . . But this hour and the power of darkness are yours" (Luke 22:52-53). The power of darkness is Satan. Jesus was saying, "This is the hour for My judgment on you and the power of darkness." He regarded the cross as a conflict with Satan. Satan would bruise Jesus on the heel, but Jesus would crush Satan's head (cf. Genesis 3:15).

He had become incarnate with the express purpose of destroying the devil. Hebrews 2:14 says, "Since then the children share in flesh and blood, He Himself likewise also partook of the same, that through death He might render powerless him who had the power of death, that is, the devil." First John 3:8 says why Jesus came: "The Son of God appeared for this purpose, that He might destroy the works of the devil." Jesus looked at the cross as a conflict with the devil, and He knew He would be victorious.

Since the cross, the power of Satan has been broken. He is still active, but he has been stunned. Soon, he will be cast into the lake of fire. Because he has already had his power broken, he has no power in your life unless you yield to him. Now he is the prisoner of Christ and will be cast into hell.

So in effect Jesus was saying to His disciples, "Look at the cross from My perspective. I am through battling Satan; I've had enough of being beaten and buffeted; I'm finished with this endless conflict. When I go to the cross, I'm going to destroy the devil. You should not grieve but be joyful. I'm going to defeat the archenemy, who has troubled us for ages." Satan's schemes to get Jesus to the cross were only part of God's plan to destroy His enemy.

Satan tried desperately but in vain to find a place where Jesus was vulnerable. Jesus said in verse 30, "The ruler of the world . . . has nothing in Me." Satan had looked for some sin that would make a weak point, but he could not find one because Jesus had none.

If Satan had been able to find any sin in Christ, our Lord would have been worthy of death. As Romans 6:23 says, "The wages of sin is death." But Hebrews 4:15 says that we have a high priest "who has been tempted in all things as we are, yet without sin." In the words of Hebrews 7:26, "It was fitting that we should have such a high priest, holy, innocent, undefiled, separated from sinners and exalted above the heavens." He did not sin; He could not sin. Satan had entered into conflict with One who was not vulnerable. And it was Satan who would be destroyed.

HIS LOVE WOULD BE DEMONSTRATED

If Jesus did nothing to deserve death, we are left wondering why He was allowed to die. The answer is that Jesus wanted to demonstrate His love for the Father. He was voluntarily going to the cross so "that the world may know that I love the Father, and as the Father gave Me commandment, even so I do" (v. 31). He portrayed Himself as a Son who was obedient to His Father. Thus although it is also true that He died because He loved *us,* here He emphasizes His love for *the Father.* It was a supreme act of love to allow Satan to kill Him without legitimate reason, just because it was the Father's will that He die. Through His obedience, He showed the world how He loved the Father.

It is interesting that although Jesus often spoke of His obedience to the Father, this is the only time in the New Testament He specifically affirms His *love* for the Father. Yet each mention of His obedience implies His love.

The religious leaders of His day all claimed to love God. But theirs was a superficial imitation of love, because it could not pass the test of obedience. Jesus has said three times in this chapter that the test of love is obedience (verses 15, 21, and 23). Now He gives them living proof of His love: He would die because that was the Father's plan. He would die because He loved the Father — not because He deserved it, but because God had designed it. He wanted to show the world His love for the Father, and He rejoiced at the opportunity, for love is shown best in selfless, sacrificial service for the one loved.

You would think that as the disciples listened and learned what Jesus' death meant to Him, surely they would have been jolted out of their selfish stupor. They had a difficult few days ahead, and their pain might have been greatly eased if they could have begun to see through Jesus' eyes. He wanted them to understand the grandeur of the scheme of salvation that was unfolding all around them. If only they had listened, they might have been able to see beyond their little, selfish sense of sorrow and loneliness. But that did not happen until after the resurrection.

We tend to be like the disciples — concerned about our own problems and needs. Many times our prayers are full of asking but void of thanks. We beg but do not praise. Instead of looking at things selfishly — how they affect us — we should look at the way they affect the cause of Christ. We must pray that God will cure us of ourselves so that we can be totally obedient to the Father.

9

The Vine and the Branches

At key points in His ministry, Christ emphasized His eqaulity with God in the clearest possible terminology. The strongest affirmations of His deity employed the name God used when He first revealed Himself to Moses — "I AM" (Exodus 3:14).

Jesus had already said, "I am the bread of life" (John 6:35), "I am the light of the world" (John 8:12), "I am the door" (John 10:9), and "I am the way" (John 14:6). Now, the night before His death, in John 15:1, He tells them, "I am the . . . vine." Like the other great "I am" passages recorded in the gospel of John, it points to His deity. Each one is a metaphor that elevates Jesus to the level of Creator, Sustainer, Savior, and Lord — titles that can be claimed only by God.

> I am the true vine, and My Father is the vinedresser. Every branch in Me that does not bear fruit, He takes away; and every branch that bears fruit, He prunes it, that it may bear more fruit. You are already clean because of the word which I have spoken to you. Abide in Me, and I in you. As the branch cannot bear fruit of itself, unless it abides in the vine, so neither can you, unless you abide in Me. I am the vine, you are the branches; he who abides in Me, and I in him, he bears much fruit; for apart from Me you can do nothing. If anyone does not abide in Me, he is thrown away as a branch, and dries up; and they gather them, and cast them into the fire, and they are burned. If you abide in Me, and My words abide in you, ask whatever you wish, and it shall be done for you. By this is My Father glorified, that you bear much fruit, and so prove to be My disciples.
>
> (John 15:1-7)

The metaphor in John 15 is of a vine and its branches. The vine is the source and sustenance of life for the branches, and the branches must abide in the vine to live and bear fruit. Jesus, of course, is the vine, and the branches are people. Although it is obvious that the fruit-bearing branches represent true Christians, the identity of the fruitless ones is in question. Some Bible students say the barren branches are Christians who bear no spiritual fruit. Others believe they are non-Christians. As always, however, we must look to the context for the best answer.

The true meaning of the metaphor is made clear when we consider the characters in that night's drama. The disciples were with Jesus. He had loved them to the uttermost; He had comforted them with the words recorded in John chapter 14. The Father was foremost in His thoughts, because He was thinking of the events of the next day. But He was also aware of someone else — the betrayer. Judas had been dismissed from the fellowship when he rejected Jesus' final appeal of love.

All the characters of the drama were in the mind of Jesus. He saw the eleven, whom He loved deeply and passionately. He was aware of the Father, with whom He shared an infinite love. And He must have grieved over Judas, whom He had loved unconditionally.

All those characters play a part in Jesus' metaphor. The vine is Christ; the vinedresser is the Father. The fruit-bearing branches represent the eleven and all true disciples of the church age. The fruitless branches represent Judas and all those who never were true disciples.

Jesus had long been aware of the difference between Judas and the eleven. After washing the disciples' feet, He said, " 'He who has bathed needs only to wash his feet, but is completely clean; and you are clean, but not all of you.' For He knew the one who was betraying Him; for this reason He said, 'Not all of you are clean' " (John 13:10-11). Once a person is forgiven by God, he is clean and does not need the bathing of forgiveness again. All that is necessary is to clean the dust and dirt of daily sins from his feet.

His point was that a child of God who commits a sin does not need to be saved again; he needs only to restore his personal relationship with the Father. But Judas had not even been "bathed," because he was not a child of God, and Jesus knew it. That is why he added, "Not all of you are clean."

Judas appeared to be like the other disciples. He was with Jesus the same amount of time — he had even been given the responsibility of keeping the money. It appeared that he was a branch like the others — but he never bore real fruit. God finally removed that branch from the vine, and it was burned.

Some would say he had lost his salvation. According to them, the same could happen to any believer who does not bear fruit. But Jesus made a promise to His children: "I give eternal life to them, and they shall never perish; and no one shall snatch them out of My hand" (John 10:28). He guaranteed the security of the child of God: "All that the Father gives Me shall come to Me, and the one who comes to Me I will certainly not cast out" (John 6:37). A true believer cannot lose his salvation and be condemned to hell.

A branch that is truly connected to the vine is secure and will never be removed. But one that only *appears* to be connected — one that has only a superficial connection — will be removed. If it does not have the life of the vine flowing through it, no fruit will be borne. Those are the Judas-branches.

There are people who, like Judas, appear by human perception to be united with Christ, but they are apostates doomed to hell. They may attend church, know all the right answers, and go through religious motions; but God will remove them, and they will be burned. Others, like the eleven, are genuinely connected to the vine and bear fruit.

CHRIST IS THE TRUE VINE

Jesus was not introducing a new idea by using the metaphor of a vine and branches. In the Old Testament, God's vine was Israel. He used the Israelites to accomplish His purpose in the world, and He blessed those connected with them. He was the vinedresser; He cared for the vine, trimmed it, and cut off branches that did not bear fruit.

But God's vine degenerated and bore no fruit. The vinedresser grieved over the tragedy of Israel's fruitlesness:

> Let me sing now for my well-beloved
> A song of my beloved concerning His vineyard.
> My well-beloved had a vineyard on a fertile hill.
> And He dug it all around, removed its stones,
> And planted it with the choicest vine.
> And He built a tower in the middle of it,
> And hewed out a wine vat in it;
> Then He expected it to produce good grapes,
> But it produced only worthless ones.

"And now, O inhabitants of Jerusalem and men of Judah,
Judge between Me and My vineyard.
What more was there to do for My vineyard that I have not done
    in it?
Why, when I expected it to produce good grapes did it produce
    worthless ones?
So now let Me tell you what I am going to do to My vineyard:
I will remove its hedge and it will be consumed;
I will break down its wall and it will become trampled ground.
And I will lay it waste;
It will not be pruned or hoed,
But briars and thorns will come up.
I will also charge the clouds to rain no rain on it."

For the vineyard of the Lord of Hosts is the house of Israel.
                                                            (Isaiah 5:1-7a)

God had done everything He could to make Israel bear fruit, yet it bore none. So He took away its wall and left it unprotected. It was then trampled down by foreign nations and laid waste. Israel was no longer God's vine; it had forfeited its privilege.

Now there is a new vine. No longer does blessing come through a covenantal relationship with Israel. Fruit and blessing come through connection with Jesus Christ.

Jesus is the true vine. In Scripture, the word *true* is often used to describe what is eternal, heavenly, and divine. Israel was imperfect, but Christ is perfect; Israel was the type, but Christ is the reality.

He is also the "true tabernacle," as opposed to the original, earthly Tabernacle (Hebrews 8:2). He is the "true light" (John 1:9). God revealed His light before, but Christ is the perfect light; He is all that can be revealed. He is also the "true bread" (John 6:32). God had sustained men by manna from heaven, but Christ is the highest quality of bread, the perfect sustenance.

Jesus chose the figure of a vine for several reasons. The lowliness of a vine demonstrates His humility. It also pictures a close, permanent, vital union between the vine and branches. It is symbolic of belonging, because branches belong entirely to the vine; if branches are to live and bear fruit, they must completely depend on the vine for nourishment, support, strength, and vitality.

Yet many who call themselves Christians fail to depend on Christ. Instead of being attached to the true vine, they are tied to a bank account. Others are attached to their education. Some have tried to make vines out of popularity, fame, personal skills, possessions, relationships, or fleshly desires. Some think the church is their vine and try to attach themselves to a religious system. But none of those things can sustain or bear fruit. The vine is Christ.

THE FATHER IS THE VINEDRESSER

In the metaphor, Christ is a plant, but the Father is a person. Certain false teachers have claimed that this aspect of the metaphor shows that Christ is not divine but lower in character and essence than the Father. They say that if He is God, His and the Father's parts in the metaphor should be equal; He should be the vine, and the Father should be the root of the vine.

But to make such a claim is to miss the whole point of Jesus' metaphor and the reason the apostle John included it in his gospel. Although He is affirming His equality in essence with the Father — by claiming to be the source and sustainer of life — He is also emphasizing the fundamental difference in His role and that of the Father's. The point is that the Father cares for the Son and for those joined to the Son by faith.

The disciples were familiar with the role of the vinedresser. After a vine is planted, the vinedresser has two duties. First, he cuts off fruitless branches, which take away sap from the fruit-bearing branches. If sap is wasted, the plant will bear less fruit. Then, he constantly trims shoots from the fruit-bearing branches so that all the sap is concentrated on fruit-bearing. Both of those duties are described in verse 2: "Every branch in Me that does not bear fruit, He takes away; and every branch that bears fruit, He prunes it, that it may bear more fruit."

The fruitless branches that are cut off are useless. Because they do not burn well, they cannot be used even to warm a house. They are thrown into piles and burned like garbage. As verse 2 says, they are "taken away." He doesn't repair them; He removes them.

Those who are removed only *appear* to be connected to Christ. They do not really abide in the vine. They were never saved. They are Judas-branches that do not really follow Jesus, and they bear no fruit. At some point in time, the Father removes them to preserve the life and fruitfulness of the other branches.

The fruit-bearing branches are pruned so that they will bear more fruit. We know these branches represent Christians, because only Christians can bear fruit. Pruning is not done only once — it is a constant process. The Father prunes a branch so that it can bear more fruit. After continual pruning, it bears much fruit. As verse 8 says, "By this is My Father glorified, that you bear much fruit."

THE FRUITLESS BRANCHES ARE REMOVED

Fruit-bearing and non-fruit-bearing branches grow rapidly and must be carefully pruned. If there is to be a large quantity of fruit, the fruitless branches must be removed as well as the shoots that grow on the fruit-bearing branches.

In first-century Palestine, it was common to prevent a vine from bearing fruit for three years after it was planted. In the fourth year it was strong enough to bear fruit. Its fruit-bearing capacity had been increased by careful pruning. Mature branches, which had already been through the four-year process, were pruned annually between December and January.

Jesus said His followers were like mature branches that bore fruit but needed pruning. There is no such thing as a fruitless Christian. Every Christian bears *some* fruit. You may have to look hard to find even a small grape, but if you look close enough, you will find something.

It is the essence of the Christian life to bear fruit. Ephesians 2:10 says, "For we are His workmanship, created in Christ Jesus for good works, which God prepared beforehand, that we should walk in them." The fruit of salvation is good works. James 2:17 explains the close relationship between faith and works: "Even so faith, if it has no works, is dead, being by itself." If saving faith is legitimate, it produces fruit. That does not mean a person is saved by works but that works are evidence that faith is genuine.

Jesus says that a genuine believer can be tested by his fruit. In Matthew 7:16-17, He says, "You will know them by their fruits. Grapes are not gathered from thorn bushes, nor figs from thistles, are they? Even so, *every* good tree bears good fruit; but the bad tree bears bad fruit" (emphasis added). If a person's faith is genuine, his life will bear good fruit. Jesus' illustration would make no sense if every Christian does not bear at least some fruit.

John the Baptist recognized the connection between salvation and fruit-bearing. When he saw the Pharisees and Sadducees coming to be baptized, he said, "You brood of vipers, who warned you to flee from the wrath to come? Therefore bring forth fruit in keeping with your repentance" (Luke 3:7-8). Lack of fruit showed that their repentance was not genuine.

Since all Christians bear fruit, it is clear that the fruitless branches in John 15 cannot refer to them. In fact, the fruitless branches had to be eliminated and thrown into the fire. Yet, in verse 2, Jesus refers to the fruitless branches as those who are "in Me." If they are "in Him," are they not genuine believers?

Not necessarily. Other passages in Scripture show it is possible to be a parasite on the vine, seemingly a part of it, but only in appearance. For example, Romans 9:6 says, "For they are not all Israel who are descended from Israel." A person can be part of the nation of Israel yet not be a true Israelite. Likewise, one can be a branch without abiding in the true vine. In a similar metaphor, Romans 11:17-24 represents Israel as an olive tree from which God has removed branches. Those branches were cut off because of unbelief (Romans 11:20).

Some only appear to be a part of God's people. Luke 8:18 says, "Therefore take care how you listen; for whoever has, to him shall more be given; and whoever does not have, even what he thinks he has shall be taken away from him." Those who only appear to belong will be removed from God's people.

Clearly, some who *appear* to be in Christ do not truly abide in Him. As 1 John 2:19 says, "They went out from us, but they were not really of us; for if they had been of us, they would have remained with us; but they went out, in order that it might be shown that they all are not of us."

If you are religious, you need to be sure your connection to Christ is genuine. The apostle Paul said, "Test yourselves to see if you are in the faith; examine yourselves! Or do you not recognize this about yourselves, that Jesus Christ is in you — unless indeed you fail the test?" (2 Corinthians 13:5).

We have a stern warning from Scripture to check our own lives and make sure our salvation is genuine. This is serious; a branch that does not bear fruit is taken away and burned. Those who say the discarded branches are Christians have a problem: the branches are burned. If they are Christians, it would mean they have lost their salvation forever.

But those fruitless branches are Judas-branches, false branches, people who associate themselves with Jesus and His people and put on a facade of faith in Him. But even though they may appear to be connected to Christ, their association is superficial. So the Father removes them.

THE FRUITFUL BRANCHES ARE PRUNNED

Although the fruitless branches are removed from the vine and burned, the Father tenderly cares for the fruit-bearing branches. In verse 2, Jesus tells His disciples, "Every branch that bears fruit, He prunes it, that it may bear more fruit." *All* the fruit-bearing branches are included. The vinedresser prunes the branches so that they will bear *much* fruit.

Kathairō is the original Greek word for "prune," or "cleanse." In farming, it referred to cleaning the husks off corn and cleaning the soil before planting crops. In the metaphor of the vine, it refers to cleaning shoots off branches.

In first-century Palestine, vinedressers removed shoots in several ways. Sometimes the tip was pinched off so that the shoot would grow more slowly. Larger branches were topped to prevent them from becoming too long and weak. Unwanted flower or grape clusters were thinned out.

Prunning is necessary in our spiritual lives. The Father removes sins and the superfluous things that limit our fruitfulness. One of the best ways to cleanse us is to allow suffering and problems to come into our lives. He prunes us with a vinedresser's knife. Sometimes it hurts, and we wonder if He knows what He is doing. It may seem we are the only branch getting pruned, though other branches need it more. But the vinedresser knows what He is doing.

Spiritual pruning can take many forms. It may be sickness, hardship, or loss of material possessions. It may be persecution or slander from non-Christians. For some it is the loss of a loved one or grief in a relationship. Or it may be a combination of difficulties. Whatever the method, the effect is to narrow our focus and strengthen the quality of our fruit.

Whatever method of pruning God uses, we can be assured He cares about us and wants us to bear much fruit. He wants to free us from the shoots that drain our life and energy. He continues His care throughout our lives to keep us spiritually healthy and productive.

Knowing the Father's love and concern should change the way we look at trials. He does not allow us to experience problems and struggles for no purpose. The problems He permits are designed to develop us so that we can bear more fruit.

He does that because He loves us. As Hebrews 12:6 says, "For those whom the Lord loves He disciplines, and He scourges every son whom He receives."

Do you look at trials and problems as pruning done by our loving Vinedresser? Or do you lapse into self-pity, fear, complaining, and brooding? Perhaps you feel God has good intentions but just does not know what He is doing. Or maybe you ask, "God, why me? Why do I have problems when it seems like no one else does?"

If we remember that God is trying to make us more fruitful, we can look past the pruning process to the goal. It is thrilling to realize that God wants our lives to bear much fruit. Hebrews 12:7 encourages us to have a proper perspective on God's perfecting process: "It is for discipline that you endure; God deals with you as with sons; for what son is there whom his father does not discipline?"

In Hebrews 12:10, the writer goes on to emphasize that this discipline is for our good: "For they [our earthly fathers] disciplined us for a short time as seemed best to them, but He disciplines us for our good, that we may share His holiness." The pruning process hurts, but the fruit — holiness — is well worth it.

The vinedresser's pruning knife is the Word of God. In verse 3, Jesus says to the disciples, "You are already clean because of the word which I have spoken to you." The word translated "clean" in that verse is the same word He used in verse 2 to describe the pruning process. God's Word cleans the sin out of our lives. That stimulates fruitfulness.

The Father uses affliction to make us more responsive to His Word. Most of us become more sensitive to the truth of Scripture when we are in trouble. When we have a particular problem, a verse of Scripture sometimes will seem to jump off the page. In adversity, the Word of God comes alive.

Spurgeon said, "The Word is often the knife with which the great Husbandman prunes the vine; and, brothers and sisters, if we were more willing to feel the edge of the Word, and to let it cut away even something that may be very dear to us, we should not need so much pruning by affliction. It is because that first knife does not always produce the desired result that another sharp tool is used by which we are effectually pruned."[1]

The pruning process helps us bear more fruit. If there is no fruit in your life, if there is no genuine connection to Jesus Christ, you are in danger of being removed and cast into the fire of hell. If there is fruit in your life, you can rejoice that affliction is making the pruning knife more effective and that the Vinedresser's ultimate goal is that you bear much fruit.

1. C. H. Spurgeon, *Spurgeon's Expository Encyclopedia*, vol. 4 (Grand Rapids: Baker, 1977), p. 337.

10

Abiding in Christ

Our relationship to Christ is unlike anything else in the human realm. It can be described only by comparing it to relationships with which we are familiar. It is like a deep friendship. It is like two people in love with each other or like the love and respect shared by a father and son.

Scripture uses a number of metaphors to describe our relationship to Christ. He is the King, and we are the subjects; He is the Shepherd, and we are the sheep; He is the Head, and we are the body. One of the best metaphors is the one Christ Himself used in John 15:1-11, where He is the vine, and we are the branches:

> I am the true vine, and My Father is the vinedresser. Every branch in Me that does not bear fruit, He takes away; and every branch that bears fruit, He prunes it, that it may bear more fruit. You are already clean because of the word which I have spoken to you. Abide in Me, and I in you. As the branch cannot bear fruit of itself, unless it abides in the vine, so neither can you, unless you abide in Me. I am the vine, you are the branches; he who abides in Me, and I in him, he bears much fruit; for apart from Me you can do nothing. If anyone does not abide in Me, he is thrown away as a branch, and dries up; and they gather them, and cast them into the fire, and they are burned. If you abide in Me, and My words abide in you, ask whatever you wish, and it shall be done for you. By this is My Father glorified, that you bear much fruit, and so prove to be My disciples. Just as the Father has loved Me, I have also loved you; abide in My love. If you keep My commandments,

you will abide in My love; just as I have kept My Father's commandments, and abide in His love. These things I have spoken to
you, that My joy may be in you, and that your joy may be made
full.

The vine-and-branches concept makes an ideal metaphor, because it is filled with parallels to our relationship with Christ. A
branch grows through its connection with the vine, and we grow
because of our relationship with Christ. A branch is nothing apart
from the vine, and we can do nothing apart from Him. A branch
draws strength from the vine, and we become strong through Him.

In the metaphor of John 15, Christ is the vine, and the Father is
the vinedresser. He prunes the fruit-bearing branches to make
them bear more fruit. He removes the fruitless branches, and they
are burned. Through continual pruning, the fruitfulness of the
vine is increased. The branches that abide in the vine — those who
are truly in Christ — are blessed, they grow and bear fruit, and the
Father lovingly tends them. It is a beautiful picture of the Christian
life, and it magnifies the blessings associated with abiding in Christ:
salvation, fruitfulness, answered prayer, abundant life, full joy, and
security.

SALVATION

The branches that abide in the true vine represent those who are
truly saved. The others are not properly connected to the vine. You
have seen shrubs that have weeds growing in them. The weeds are
intertwined with the branches of the shrubs and appear to be part
of the same plant, but in reality they are attached to a different
root. They are like people who have only a superficial relation to
Christ.

Tragically, some people pretend to be Christians but have no real
connection to Christ. They might go to church regularly or be involved in a Bible study. They might even talk about having a relationship with Jesus. But they are not genuine branches in the vine.
Evangelical churches are filled with false branches. Some husbands
come to church only because their wives want them to. Some young
people come to church to be involved in a youth program, but they
are not interested in knowing Christ personally. In fact, many out-
wardly spiritual people never go beyond mere association with
Christians.

Jesus pleads with people who are superficial branches. He says in
verse 4, "Abide in Me." He is saying to those who are like Judas, "Be

genuine; abide in Me and show that your faith is real; bear fruit and remain on the vine." It is like saying, "You superficial branches: be saved; have a genuine relation to Christ."

Abiding in Christ is a mark of true salvation. Sometimes a person who is active in the church leaves suddenly and never again returns. Or a leader in the church may become apostate. People in the church wonder what happened. The explanation is in 1 John 2:19: "They went out from us, but they were not really of us; for if they had been of us, they would have remained with us; but they went out, in order that it might be shown that they all are not of us."

If a person's relationship to Christ is genuine, he remains. First John 2:24-25 says, "As for you, let that abide in you which you heard from the beginning. If what you heard from the beginning abides in you, you also will abide in the Son and in the Father. And this is the promise which He Himself made to us: eternal life." Those who abide inherit eternal life.

That is not to say that you can be saved by being steadfast. The point is that if you continue in the faith, you are showing that your connection to Christ is real; if you depart, you demonstrate that it never was.

Paul makes the same point in Colossians 1:22-23: "He has now reconciled you in His fleshly body through death, in order to present you before Him holy and blameless and beyond reproach — if indeed you continue in the faith firmly established and steadfast, and not moved away from the hope of the gospel that you have heard, which was proclaimed in all creation under heaven."

Hebrews 3:6 likewise says, "Christ was faithful as a Son over His house whose house we are, if we hold fast our confidence and the boast of our hope firm until the end." By continuing in Christ we give evidence that we are really part of His household. Hebrews 3 says, "For we have become partakers of Christ, if we hold fast the beginning of our assurance firm until the end" (v. 14). A true believer has a living and vital relationship with Jesus Christ that cannot give way to unbelief or apostasy.

Only the person who abides in the true vine can claim the promise of the constant presence of God. Jesus said, "Abide in Me, and I in you" (v. 4). That means that if we truly abide in Him, He will truly abide within us.

Many people come to church thinking that God is with them just because they sit in the pew. But being in a church does not mean that the Lord is with you. He does not live inside a church; He lives in His disciples. A person who sits among true disciples might be as far from Christ as the native of a tribe that has never heard the gospel — if he does not abide in the true vine.

Jesus says in verse 9, "Just as the Father has loved Me, I have also loved you; abide in My love." A real disciple doesn't come to Christ, receive His love, and then leave again; he remains. That is what Jesus is saying, whether he says "abide," "bear much fruit," or "abide in My love." They all mean, "Be a real believer."

A Christian can abide only by being firmly grounded in Jesus. If a branch is to abide, it cannot be even half an inch away — it must be connected. Those who are saved are those who are abiding, and those who are not abiding are not saved.

FRUITFULNESS

Those who truly abide will bear fruit. Jesus tells us how in verse 4: "Abide in Me, and I in you. As the branch cannot bear fruit of itself, unless it abides in the vine, so neither can you, unless you abide in Me." The person who abides discovers that his soul is nourished with the truths of God as he stays in a close, living, energized relationship with Jesus Christ. The natural result is spiritual fruit.

Sometimes we think we can bear fruit alone. We become independent because we think we are strong or clever. Or sometimes we look at fruit we have borne in the past and think we can do it alone; we forget God worked through us to produce that fruit.

A branch can bear no fruit apart from the vine. Even strong branches cannot bear fruit independent of the vine. Cut off from the vine, even the strongest branches become as helpless as the weakest; the most beautiful are as helpless as the ugliest; and the best are as worthless as the worst.

Fruit-bearing is not a matter of being strong or weak, good or bad, brave or cowardly, clever or foolish, experienced or inexperienced. Whatever your gifts, accomplishments, or virtues, they cannot produce fruit if you are detached from Jesus Christ.

Christians who think they are bearing fruit apart from the vine are only tying on artificial fruit. They run around grunting and groaning to produce fruit but accomplish nothing. Fruit is borne not by trying but by abiding.

To bear genuine fruit, you must take your place on the vine and get as close to Jesus as you can. Strip away all the things of the world. Put aside the sins that distract you and sap your energy. Put aside everything that robs you of a deep, personal, loving relationship with Jesus. Stay apart from sin, and be in God's Word.

Having done all that, do not worry about bearing fruit. It is not your concern. The vine will merely use you to bear fruit. Get close to Jesus Christ, and His energy in you will bear fruit.

Some people find reading the Bible insipid and boring; they think sharing their faith is dull. Others find those things exciting. Invariably, the difference is that one is working on the deeds, and the other is concentrating on his relationship with Jesus Christ. Don't focus on the deeds; focus on your walk with Christ. The deeds will grow naturally out of your relationship.

Fruit is a frequent metaphor in Scripture. The main word for it is used approximately one hundred times in the Old Testament and seventy times in the New Testament; it appears in twenty-four of the twenty-seven New Testament books. It is mentioned often, yet it is often misunderstood.

Fruit is not outward success. Many people think that if a ministry is big and involves a great many people, it is fruitful. But a church or Bible study group is not successful just because it has many people — fleshly effort can produce big numbers. Some missionaries might minister to few people but bear much fruit.

Fruit-bearing is not sensationalism. A person does not have a great deal of fruit because he is enthusiastic or can make others enthusiastic about a church program. God produces real fruit in our lives when we abide.

The fruit of the Spirit is common to all of us, yet the Spirit uses each person differently. Fruit cannot be produced by simulating the genuine fruit another person has borne. It is tempting to see the fruit another person has produced and try to duplicate it. Instead of abiding, we try to produce what someone else has produced but end up with only artificial fruit. God did not design us to produce the same kind of fruit as another. Our fruit is uniquely arranged, ordered, and designed.

CHRISTLIKE CHARACTER

Real fruit is, first of all, Christlike character. A believer who is like Christ bears fruit. That is what Paul means in Galatians 5:22-23 when he says, "But the fruit of the Spirit is love, joy, peace, patience, kindness, goodness, faithfulness, gentleness, self-control; against such things there is no law." Those were all characteristics of Christ.

Christlike character is not produced by self-effort. It grows naturally out of a relationship with Christ. We don't first try to be loving, and when we have become loving, try to be joyful, and so on. Instead, those qualities become part of our lives as we abide in Christ by staying close to Him.

THANKFUL PRAISE

Second, thankful praise to God is fruit. Hebrews 13:15 says, "Through Him then, let us continually offer up a sacrifice of praise to God, that is, the fruit of lips that give thanks to His name." When you praise God and thank Him for who He is and what He has done, you offer Him fruit.

HELP TO THOSE IN NEED

Help to those in need is a third kind of fruit to God. When the Philippian church gave Paul a gift, he told them he was glad for their sake that they had: "Not that I seek the gift itself, but I seek for the profit which increases to your account" (Philippians 4:17). He appreciated what they had given, not for the sake of the gift, but for the fruit in their lives.

Paul told the Romans: "Therefore, when I have finished this, and have put my seal on this fruit of theirs, I will go on by way of you to Spain" (Romans 15:28). Again he referred to a gift as "fruit." In both cases, the gift revealed the love of the ones who gave it, so Paul counted the gifts as fruit. A gift to someone in need is fruit if it is offered from a loving heart in the divine energy of the indwelling Christ.

PURITY IN CONDUCT

Purity in conduct is another kind of spiritual fruit. Paul wanted Christians to be holy in their behavior, to " walk in a manner worthy of the Lord, to please Him in all respects, bearing fruit in every good work and increasing in the knowledge of God," as he put it in Colossians 1:10.

CONVERTS

Converts are another type of fruit. Many New Testament passages show that converts are spiritual fruit. For example, in 1 Corinthians 16:15, Paul calls the first converts in Achaia the "first fruits of Achaia."

Like other spiritual fruit, success in winning converts is not accomplished by anxiously running around. It comes by abiding in the vine. The way to be effective in leading people to Christ is not solely by being aggressive; rather it is by abiding in Christ. Concentrate on your relationship to Jesus Christ, and He will give you opportunities to speak of your faith. There is no need to become anxious because you have not yet won a certain number of people to

Christ. As you become closer to Him and more like Him, you will discover that sharing your faith is a natural outgrowth of abiding. You may not always see fruit immediately, but fruit will be borne, nevertheless.

When Jesus was traveling to Samaria, He met a woman getting water. She told the people in her town about Jesus. As the people from the town came out to meet Him, He said to the disciples,

> Lift up your eyes, and look on the fields, that they are white for harvest. Already he who reaps is receiving wages, and is gathering fruit for life eternal; that he who sows and he who reaps may rejoice together. For in this case the saying is true, "One sows, and another reaps." I sent you to reap that for which you have not labored; others have labored, and you have entered into their labor.
> (John 4:35-38)

The disciples were reaping the fruits of other people's labor. Those people did not see all the results of their labor, but their efforts still bore fruit.

William Carey spent thirty-five years in India before he saw one convert. Some people think he led a fruitless life. But almost every convert in India to this day is fruit on his branch, because he translated the whole New Testament into many different Indian dialects. He was not the one to reap what he had sown, but his life bore much fruit.

One of the most fulfilling experiences in life is to bear fruit for God. If that is not happening in your life, the reason is simple — you are not abiding in the vine.

ANSWERED PRAYER

God gives an incredible promise to those who abide: "If you abide in Me, and My words abide in you, ask whatever you wish, and it shall be done for you" (v. 7).

Notice that there are two conditions to that promise. First, we must abide. The Greek word for *abide* is in the aorist tense; it indicates something that happened at one point in time and has permanent results. Again, it refers to salvation and indicates that the promise is only for real believers.

Of course, in His sovereign wisdom, God sometimes answers the prayers of a non-Christian; but He does not obligate Himself to do so. If He does, it is His sovereign choice and for His purpose; but He does not have to. The promise of answered prayer is reserved only for those who abide in the true Vine.

Still, many who are true branches do not always get answers to their prayers. That may be because they are not meeting Jesus' second condition: "If . . . *My words* abide in you" (v. 7, emphasis added).

"My words" does not mean only the individual words of Christ. Some people use red-letter Bibles incorrectly because they regard the words of Jesus as more inspired or more important than the words of other writers of Scripture. But the words of Paul, Peter, John, and Jude are just as important. The Lord Jesus Christ has spoken through all of Scripture; it is all His message to us. Therefore, when He says, "If My words abide in you," He means we must have such high regard for all of Scripture that we let it abide in us, that we hide it in our hearts, and that we commit ourselves to knowing and obeying it.

To meet the first condition, abiding in Christ, a person must be a Christian. To meet the second condition, abiding in His Word, a person must study all of Scripture in order to govern his life by that which Christ revealed.

The same principle is found in John 14:14: "If you ask Me anything in My name, I will do it." Praying in His name is not merely adding "in Jesus' name" to the end of a prayer. It means praying for that which is consistent with the words and will of Christ.

The Christian who is abiding in Christ and who is controlled by His Word is not going to ask anything against God's will. Because he wants what God wants, he is guaranteed an answer to his prayer.

Our prayers often go unanswered because we pray selfishly. James 4:3 says, "You ask and do not receive, because you ask with wrong motives, so that you may spend it on your pleasures."

Our prayers will be answered if we follow Paul's example in 2 Corinthians 10:5: "We are destroying speculations and every lofty thing raised up against the knowledge of God, and we are taking every thought captive to the obedience of Christ." We must rid our minds of everything that violates God's truth and will. When we think according to the will of God, we will pray according to the will of God, and our prayers will be answered.

There is so little power in the prayers of the church today because we are not fully abiding and seeking His mind. Instead of bringing our minds into obedience to Christ and asking according to His will, we ask selfishly, and, as a result, our prayers go unanswered. If we cultivated an intimate love relationship with Christ, we would desire what He desires, and we would ask and receive.

The psalmist said, "Delight yourself in the Lord; and He will give you the desires of your heart" (Psalm 37:4). That means that when you delight completely in the Lord, He implants the right desires in your heart. His desires become yours. What a blessing it is to know that God will answer every prayer we bring to Him!

ABUNDANT LIFE

Abiding in Christ is the source of the abundant life Jesus spoke of in John 10:10. Those who abide fulfill the magnificent purpose of life, which is to give God the glory He deserves. Jesus says in verse 8, "By this is My Father glorified, that you bear much fruit." When a Christian abides, God can work through him to produce much fruit. Since God produces it, He is the One glorified.

Paul recognized the source of fruit in his life. In Romans 15:18 he says, "For I will not presume to speak of anything except what Christ has accomplished through me." He did not tell people how good he was at preaching or evangelism. He recognized that everything worthwhile in his life came from God. In Galatians 2:20 he says, "I have been crucified with Christ; and it is no longer I who live, but Christ lives in me." He knew God did it all.

Peter has the same idea in mind in 1 Peter 2:12: "Keep your behavior excellent among the Gentiles, so that in the thing in which they slander you as evildoers, they may on account of your good deeds, as they observe them, glorify God in the day of visitation."

So this is the logical progression: The one who abides bears fruit; God is glorified in the fruit because He is the One who deserves credit for it; the purpose of life is fulfilled because God is glorified; and thus the one who so abides and glorifes God experiences abundant life.

FULL JOY

One of the chief elements of the abundant life is fullness of joy, which is an outgrowth of abiding in the true vine. Jesus says in verse 11, "These things I have spoken to you, that My joy may be in you, and that your joy may be full."

God wants us to be consumed with joy, but few Christians are. Churches have many people who are bitter, discontent, and complaining. Some people think the Christian life is monastic deprivation and drudgery — a bitter religious pill. But God has designed it for our joy. It is when we violate God's design that we lose our joy. If we abide fully, we will have full joy.

When David sinned, he no longer sensed the presence of God. He cries out in Psalm 51:12, "Restore to me the joy of Thy salvation." He had allowed sin to hinder the pure abiding relationship.

He did not lose his salvation, but he lost the joy of his salvation.

That joy returned when he confessed his sin and accepted the consequences of it. His guilt was removed; he returned to a pure, unhindered, abiding relationship; and his joy was made full again.

The joy of abiding in the true vine is unaffected by external circumstances, persecution, or the disappointments of life. We can experience the same joy Jesus had. He maintained joy in spite of all the abuse He faced. And His joy flows through those who abide in Him.

SECURITY

Abiding in the true Vine brings the deepest kind of security. Romans 8:1 says, "There is therefore now no condemnation for those who are in Christ Jesus." Those who are in Him cannot be removed, they cannot be cut off, and they need not fear judgment. There is no suggestion here that those who now abide might later cease to do so. Their position is secure.

On the other hand, those who do not abide *will* be judged. Jesus says in verse 6, "If anyone does not abide in Me, he is thrown away as a branch, and dries up; and they gather them, and cast them into the fire, and they are burned." He is referring to the Judas-branches, the false disciples. Since they have no living connection to Jesus Christ, they are cast out.

The true believer can never be thrown away. Jesus promises in John 6:37, "All that the Father gives Me shall come to Me, and the one who comes to Me I will certainly not cast out." If a person is cast forth, it is because he was never a real believer.

The branches that are cast off are gathered and burned. They burn forever and ever. It is a tragic picture of God's judgment.

The parable of the wheat and the tares tells us that the angels of God gather those destined for judgment. Jesus says in Matthew 13:41-42, "The Son of Man will send forth His angels, and they will gather out of His kingdom all stumbling blocks, and those who commit lawlessness, and will cast them into the furnace of fire; in that place there shall be weeping and gnashing of teeth."

There will be a day when God sends His angels to gather from around the world the Judas-branches who have no connection to Christ. He will cast them into eternal hell. It is tragic when a person appears to be a genuine branch but ends up in hell.

William Pope was a member of the Methodist church in England for most of his life. He made a pretense of knowing Christ and served in many capacities. His wife died a genuine believer.

Soon, however, he began to drift from Christ. He had companions who believed in the redemption of demons. He began going with them to the public house of prostitution. In time, he became a drunkard.

He admired Thomas Paine, and on Sundays he and his friends assembled to confirm one another in their infidelity. They amused themselves by throwing the Bible on the floor and kicking it around.

Finally, he contracted tuberculosis. Someone visited him and told him of the great Redeemer. He said that he could be saved from the punishment of his sins.

But Pope replied, "I have no contrition; I cannot repent. God will damn me! I know the day of grace is lost. God has said to such as me, 'I will laugh at your calamity, and mock when your fear cometh.' I have denied Him; my heart is hardened."

Then he cried, "Oh, the hell, the pain I feel! I have chosen my way. I have done the horrible damnable deed: I have crucified the Son of God afresh; I have counted the blood of the covenant an unholy thing! Oh that wicked and horrible thing of blaspheming the Holy Spirit, which I know that I have committed; I want nothing but hell! Come, oh devil and take me!"[1]

He had spent his whole life in the church, but his end was infinitely worse than his beginning. Every man has the same choice. You can abide in the vine and receive all of God's blessings, or you can be burned.

It doesn't seem like a difficult choice, does it? Yet millions of people resist God's gift of salvation, prefering the superficial relationship of the false branch. Perhaps you know people like that — or perhaps you are like that yourself. If so, Jesus' plea to you is a loving invitation: "Abide in Me, and I in you."

1. John Myers, comp., *Voices from the Edge of Eternity* (Old Tappan, N. J.: Spire Books, 1972), pp. 147-49.

11

The Friends of Jesus

Ancient oriental kings often relied on a select group of advisers, special friends of the monarch, who functioned much like the cabinet of a modern American president. But these were far more than mere political consultants — they were his intimate friends. They protected and cared for him and were given immediate access to him — they could even enter his bedchamber. He valued their advice more than that of generals, statesmen, or rulers of other nations. No one was closer to the king.

Theirs was a role that transcended the king-subject or master-disciple relationship. It was a position of intimate friendship, a bond of love and trust that superseded formality, protocol, or any external threat.

Jesus cultivated that kind of relationship with His disciples, and in His final words to them on the night before He died, He repeatedly affirmed that He valued the intimacy they shared. The time had come that He must leave them, but He wanted them to be sure of their status as His friends.

> This is My commandment, that you love one another; just as I have loved you. Greater love has no one than this, that one lay down his life for his friends. You are My friends, if you do what I command you. No longer do I call you slaves, for the slave does not know what his master is doing; but I have called you friends, for all things that I have heard from My Father I have made known to you. You did not choose Me, but I chose you, and ap-

pointed you, that you should go and bear fruit, and that your fruit should remain, that whatever you ask of the Father in My name, He may give to you.

(John 15:12-16)

The Greek word for "slave," or "servant," is *doulos.* It was not viewed in the context of that culture as having a negative connotation. The disciples would have been happy to be known as Jesus' slaves. To be a servant — especially a servant of God — was by no means a shameful thing.

But to be known as the friend of God was an honor. Abraham was the only one in the Old Testament upon whom the title was conferred. Everyone familiar with the Jewish Scriptures would have been aware of the uniqueness of Abraham's place as God's friend, so Jesus' words to the eleven remaining disciples must have utterly thrilled them. All of them had longed for intimacy with Him — they had even contended among themselves about which one would sit closest to Him in the kingdom. Now He reassured all of them that He desired intimacy with them as well, and he listed a number of the characteristics essential to an intimate relationship with Him.

OBEDIENCE

The first is obedience, a characteristic that sums up the essence of friendship with Christ. In fact, obedience is a condition for intimacy. In verse 10, Jesus says, "If you keep My commandments, you will abide in My love." Then in verse 14 He adds, "You are My friends, if you do what I command you." That is not to say that friendship with Him is either earned or attained by any amount of human effort but rather that obedience is an identifying mark of the friends of Jesus.

In fact, those who obey God share intimacy with Jesus as members of the same family. Jesus had explained before that obedience is characteristic of all those in His spiritual family. Mark tells us,

And His mother and His brothers arrived, and standing outside they sent word to Him, and called Him. And a multitude was sitting around Him, and they said to Him, "Behold, Your mother and Your brothers are outside looking for You." And answering them, He said, "Who are My mother and My brothers?" And looking about on those who were sitting around Him, He said, "Behold, My mother and My brothers! For whoever does the will of God, he is My brother and sister and mother."

(Mark 3:31-35)

Scripture also speaks of the relationship of believers with Jesus as that of sheep who follow their Shepherd. Jesus says in John 10:27, "My sheep hear My voice, and I know them, and they follow Me." Again, intimacy depends on willing obedience. In fact, in every metaphor Jesus ever used to describe His relationship with His disciples, obedience was an essential condition. In John 8:31, He says, "If you abide in My word, then you are truly disciples of Mine."

Intimacy with Jesus Christ is always built on a foundation of obedience, whether it is the intimacy of a sheep and a shepherd, a teacher and a disciple, family members, or simply friends. Obedience is never optional in any relationship with Christ.

First John 3:9-10 refers to that identifying mark of the family of God: "No one who is born of God practices sin, because His seed abides in him; and he cannot sin, because he is born of God. By this the children of God and the children of the devil are obvious: any one who does not practice righteousness is not of God, nor the one who does not love his brother."

A person does not *become* a child of God through obedience — that would make salvation depend on good works. Rather, obedience is proof that a person is intimately connected to Jesus Christ through faith. It does not qualify someone to be a child of God. It only demonstrates that he is one.

The same is true of being a friend of Jesus. Verse 14 says, "You are My friends, if you do what I command you." That does not mean that obeying makes you a friend of Jesus. But if you are one, it will be visible by your obedience.

LOVE FOR EACH OTHER

A second characteristic of friendship with Jesus is love for fellow believers: "This is My commandment, that you love one another, just as I have loved you. Greater love has no one than this, that one lay down his life for his friends" (vv. 12-13). The friends of Jesus have a deep, sincere, and abiding love for other Christians.

Love is a great source of personal fulfillment, and the world is hungry for it. But friends of Jesus are the only ones who can truly experience the love the world is seeking. Non-Christians know nothing of the love believers can share, because it comes from a source they cannot know. Love is a fruit of the Spirit (Galatians 5:22). Romans 5:5 says, "The love of God has been poured out within our hearts through the Holy Spirit who was given to us." The Christian overflows with the love of God; he lives in it, and it lives in him.

You cannot be a true believer without having love for other be-lievers. The apostle John writes:

> The one who says he is in the light and yet hates his brother is in the darkness until now. The one who loves his brother abides in the light and there is no cause for stumbling in him. But the one who hates his brother is in the darkness and walks in the darkness, and does not know where he is going because the darkness has blinded his eyes.
>
> (1 John 2:9-10)

John further explains: "Whoever believes that Jesus is the Christ is born of God; and whoever loves the Father loves the child born of Him" (1 John 5:1).

That is not to say that if we ever fail to love another Christian to the fullest, it proves we are not true believers. A Christian may sometimes fail to love a brother in Christ the way he should. But John is not explaining exceptions to the rule — he is describing the general pattern believers follow.

Love is not something that needs to be learned or acquired — it is natural for a true friend of Jesus to love other friends of Jesus. Paul writes, "Now as to the love of the brethren, you have no need for anyone to write to you, for you yourselves are taught by God to love one another" (1 Thessalonians 4:9). Imperfections sometimes flaw the fellowship, but love is the general pattern. To be unloving to another Christian, a Christian has to violate his new nature in Christ, resist the love that is natural to his new nature, and conjure up sin instead.

Jesus wants us to love the way He loves. He showed His deep de-sire when He said, "This is My commandment, that you love one another, *just as I have loved you.* Greater love has no one than this, that one lay down his life for his friends" (vv. 12-13, emphasis added).

Of course our love cannot be on the same scale as His — He re-deemed the whole world. But we can love the way He loves. We can be sacrificial and selfless. We can go beyond an external love and love with a love that is total and self-giving.

No brother in Christ is a mere acquaintance. Whoever he is, we share a common spiritual heritage. We should see him as Christ sees him. Love should move us to give our wealth, to bear burdens, to feel what another feels, and to hurt where another hurts. We should be willing to comfort, to sacrifice, to instruct, and to sup-port, just the way Christ would.

The quality of our love is our testimony for Christ. Because only Christians have God's love in their lives, the world should see the greatest love in Christians. Jesus says in John 13:35, "By this all men will know that you are My disciples, if you have love for one another."

The intensity of love is revealed by the depth of sacrifice it is willing to make. Giving up one's life has always been recognized as the supreme expression of love. Jesus was about to show He had that kind of love for His disciples. He told them, "Greater love has no one than this, that one lay down his life for his friends" (v. 13).

Too many who claim to know Christ are far from sacrificing their lives — they will not even give up a few minutes of time. Money is needed for ministries around the world, but the needs go unfulfilled because many Christians do not give sacrificially. Many who say they know the Lord will not even tell someone about Him, nor will they use their spiritual gifts to help another believer grow.

Christians fall far short of dying for others. Some have not even learned how to live for others. True love requires total sacrifice. When we love the way Christ did, the world will listen to our message. It is pointless to ask nonbelievers to trust Christ when they cannot see His love operating in us.

Jesus sacrificed to the utmost, even for the unlovable. Paul says in Romans 5:7-8, "For one will hardly die for a righteous man; though perhaps for the good man someone would dare even to die. But God demonstrates His own love toward us, in that while we were yet sinners, Christ died for us."

How do you know God loves you? Because He laid down His life. It is written in 1 John 3:16, "We know love by this, that He laid down His life for us." The verse goes on to say, "We ought to lay down our lives for the brethren."

When my son Matthew was very young, he would often say to me, "I love you, Dad." I would ask him, "How much do you love me?" He would answer, "I love you big much." I would ask, "How much is big much?" He would jump into my lap, put his arms around my neck, squeeze as tight as he could, and say, "That's big much."

If we could ask God, "How much do you love me?" I believe He would answer by pointing to a rocky hillside outside Jerusalem and saying, "Do you see the cross in the middle? My Son is on it. I love you that much."

Are you ready to lay down your life for another? Do you love sacrificially? Are you caring for the needs of others? Needs are all around you. Some people need to be taught; some need reproof;

others need restoration. There are physical needs, and many people need prayer. We say we love people, but do we meet their needs?

Love is always practical. The apostle John asks, "But whoever has the world's goods, and beholds his brother in need and closes his heart against him, how does the love of God abide in him?" (1 John 3:17). He encourages the children of God to prove their love in an active way: "Little children, let us not love with word or with tongue, but in deed and truth" (1 John 3:18). The true friend of Jesus meets the needs of others.

A KNOWLEDGE OF DIVINE TRUTH

In Jesus' day, slaves and their masters rarely were friends. Not that necessarily they were enemies — they simply did not cultivate the kind of relationship friends would have. A slave was told only *what* he should do, never *why* he should do it. He never knew his master's plans, goals, or feelings. He was merely a functionary who did what he was told, a living tool rarely included in the sharing of rewards.

It was different between Jesus and His disciples. He tells them in verse 15, "No longer do I call you slaves; for the slave does not know what his master is doing; but I have called you friends, for all things that I have heard from My Father I have made known to you."

Surrender to Jesus Christ is never blind obedience. He shares with his friends everything He has received from the Father. They share His heart for His work because they know the whole plan from beginning to end. He has revealed the past, present, and future. He always makes His friends a part of His plans and purposes. It is the truest kind of friendship. We want what He wants, and we do His will because it is our heart's desire.

Jesus promised the disciples special insight. He says in John 8:31-32, "If you abide in My word, then you are truly disciples of Mine; and you shall know the truth, and the truth shall make you free." Everything the Father told Him, He passed on to them. Consider His prayer to the Father:

> I manifested Thy name to the men whom Thou gavest Me out of the world; Thine they were, and Thou gavest them to Me, and they have kept Thy word. Now they have come to know that everything Thou has given Me is from Thee; for the words which Thou gavest Me I have given to them; and they received them,

> and truly understood that I came forth from Thee, and they believed that Thou didst send Me.
>
> (John 17:6-7)

Jesus taught the disciples the mysteries of God's plan through the parables. Matthew writes, "And the disciples came and said to Him, 'Why do You speak to them in parables?' And He answered and said to them, 'To you it has been granted to know the mysteries of the kingdom of heaven, but to them it has not been granted' " (Matthew 13:10-11).

As a result, the disciples had special knowledge others sought but never found. He told them, "Blessed are the eyes which see the things you see, for I say to you, that many prophets and kings wished to see the things which you see, and did not see them, and to hear the things which you hear, and did not hear them" (Luke 10:23-24).

So spiritual knowledge has passsd from the Father through Jesus to the apostles. The apostles passed it to us through the Scriptures. Paul writes in Romans 16:25-26, "The mystery . . . has been kept secret for long ages past, but now is manifested, and by the Scriptures of the prophets, according to the commandment of the eternal God, has been made known to all the nations, leading to obedience of faith."

Spiritual understanding sets Christians apart. The things of God are spiritually discerned, and the unredeemed mind cannot understand them (1 Corinthians 2:12-16). A philosopher or scientist who seeks spiritual truth apart from the Word of God and the Spirit of God knows little compared to the simplest Christian.

Jesus did not expect His disciples to follow Him without knowing where He was leading; they were not to be enslaved to mechanical obedience. They were to be His friends, and He revealed to them the truth He could not share with those not intimate with Him.

A DIVINE APPOINTMENT

Another characteristic of Jesus' friends is that they have been chosen by God and appointed to a position of service. Friendships are usually formed when two people choose to befriend each other. But a friendship with Jesus Christ is formed when He chooses to be friends. Jesus chose twelve men to be His disciples — they did not volunteer. Luke 6:13 records, "And when day came, He called His disciples to Him; and chose twelve of them, whom He also named as apostles."

Jesus tells the disciples in verse 16, "You did not choose Me, but I chose you, and appointed you, that you should go and bear fruit, and that your fruit should remain." In verse 19 He adds, "I chose you out of the world." The Greek word for "chose" is *tithemi,* and in several places in the New Testament it is translated "to appoint," or "ordain."

Paul uses the word in 1 Corinthians 12:28, where he says, "And God has appointed in the church, first apostles, second prophets, third teachers." He uses it again in 2 Timothy 1:11, where he refers to the gospel as the message "for which I was appointed a preacher and an apostle and a teacher."

In both places, Paul is referring to being chosen to specific service. In fact, throughout Scripture, wherever the doctrine of God's sovereign choice, or election, is talked about, the context always goes beyond salvation, because whenever God elects someone to salvation, He also ordains him to special service. The friends of Jesus are not chosen just for salvation; they are chosen to do something. He tells them in verse 16, "I chose you, and appointed you, that you should go and bear fruit." We have not been chosen to stand and watch the world go by.

I was speaking at a conference of university students and met a young man who had dropped out of seminary. When I asked him what he was doing in the Lord's service, he said he was involved in a Bible study group he hoped would grow into a church. "We just have a little fellowship up here and praise God together," he said with emphasis. I asked who taught them. He replied, "Nobody teaches us; we just share. No one ever teaches." I said, "What do you feel is your purpose?" "Well," he said, "we just praise the Lord a lot."

I asked if they were involved in evangelism. "No," he said, "we've been in existence two-and-a-half years and we've never told anyone. We don't feel we are called to that. We are still an infant church, so we don't think we need to evangelize."

He had the idea they were called to sit with each other and sing. It is good to praise God and fellowship, but we are also called to go. The world will not come to us — we must go to it.

The Bible does not command those who are in the world to come to church. It commands those in the church to "go out into the highways and along the hedges, and compel them to come in" (Luke 14:23). Jesus' last commission to His followers was, "Go into all the world and preach the gospel to all creation" (Mark 16:15).

He promises the disciples in Acts 1:8, "You shall receive power when the Holy Spirit has come upon you; and you shall be My witnesses both in Jerusalem, and in all Judea and Samaria, and even to the remotest part of the earth."

Jesus chose a group of men out of the world of darkness. He saved them, loved them, and trained them. He called them His friends. Then He sent them back into the world to tell them about Jesus Christ.

We have the high calling to glorify the name of Christ in the world. We are called and ordained to let God work His perfect will through us. Thus, life has purpose for the Christian. When we communicate the gospel and a person responds by receiving Christ, we have brought about a transformation that will last for eternity. It is so different from the non-Christian, whose life dwindles away without meaning, day after day with no eternal results. The Christian's life makes ripples throughout eternity because his fruit remains. Revelation 14:13 says of the dead in Christ, "They may rest from their labors, for their deeds follow with them."

Verse 16 concludes with a promise from Jesus, "Whatever you ask of the Father in My name, He may give to you." As we have seen before, that is not a blanket promise to fulfill any request we toss up with the magic words "in Jesus' name" attached to it. It means we must ask the Father for the things Jesus would want. We cannot use prayer as a way to satisfy our lusts. We must be unselfish if we are to ask in His name. Praying in His name means asking for what He wants. If we do that, the answer is guaranteed.

We who have trusted in His name are all the friends of Jesus Christ. We are not like subjects who crowd the streets, hoping to catch a glimpse of the king as he passes by. We have the right to enter His presence any time. We are the people closest to our King. It is thrilling to know we are the personal friends of the Creator and King of the universe.

If you are not a friend of Jesus, you can be. You can know God's love for you and have a meaningful, productive life. If He is calling you to Himself — calling you to be His friend — you must respond yourself; no one else can do it for you. When you do, you will have His friendship and all that brings.

A man chooses to be the friend of Jesus Christ or the friend of the world. Friendship with the world is hostility toward God. Friendship with Jesus Christ is intimacy with God. It is fellowship with the Trinity. It is joy unspeakable and full of glory.

12

Hated Without a Cause

Several years ago, Bob Marriot, a young man from the college department at our church, was attacked and beaten while he was giving out tracts in a park. It was a brutal beating, but Bob recovered, and it was no time until he was back on the streets, telling people about Christ. He had not lost any of his zeal for the Lord.

A few weeks later Bob was speaking of Christ at Seventh and Broadway in downtown Los Angeles, at 4:40 in the afternoon, when he was attacked and beaten again. This time, the back of his skull was fractured in four places. At the hospital, doctors drilled three holes in his skill to relieve the pressure, but they were unsuccessful, and three days later Bob died. He was committed to proclaiming Christ to a Christ-hating world, and he paid for it with his life.

That incident helped to change my perspective on the cost of serving Christ in a hostile world. It is too easy to have a casual attitude toward persecution when we read about how it affects believers in other parts of the world. But when it strikes close to home, it is a much more sobering experience.

When Jesus says in Acts 1:8 that we are to be His "witnesses," He uses the Greek word *martus*, from which we get the word *martyr*. Although it originally meant "witness," so many in the early church who witnessed for Christ were killed that the word came to refer primarily to a person who died for his testimony for Christ.

Jesus wanted the disciples to know they would meet hostility when they witnessed for Him. But on the night before He died, His purpose was primarily to comfort and reassure them. The bulk of His discourse that night consisted of words of comfort and encouragement. He saved until last what He had to say about the persecution they would face after He left.

Jesus tells them of His love in chapter 13. He gives them tremendous promises in chapter 14. He promises He is going to prepare a place for them and return to take them there (vv. 2-3); tells them that they will do greater works than He has done (v. 12); says that they can ask anything in His name and He will do it (v. 13); promises that the Holy Spirit will live in them and be their Comforter (v. 16, KJV); reassures them that they will be intensely loved by Him and by the Father (v. 23); says that the disciples will possess divine life and knowledge (v. 26); and promises that He will give His peace (v. 27).

In the first portion of chapter 15, He tells them that they will bear fruit for God (v. 5). He says that they will abide and be closely connected to Him (v. 10); that they will have His joy (v. 11); and that His life will flow through them. Finally, He calls them His friends (v. 14).

Then He had to warn them. They needed to know that life would not be blissful in spite of the wonderful promises that would be fulfilled in their lives. Ministry would not be easy in a rebellious, Christ-hating world. The world was going to treat them the same way it treated Him, and they were going to be despised and persecuted — even killed.

> This I command you, that you love one another. If the world hates you, you know that it has hated Me before it hated you. If you were of the world, the world would love its own; but because you are not of the world, but I chose you out of the world, therefore the world hates you. Remember the word that I said to you, "A slave is not greater than his master." If they persecuted Me, they will also persecute you; if they kept My word, they will keep yours also. But all these things they will do to you for My name's sake, because they do not know the One who sent Me. If I had not come and spoken to them, they would not have sin, but now they have no excuse for their sin. He who hates Me hates My Father also. If I had not done among them the works which no one else did, they would not have sin; but now they have both seen and hated Me and My Father as well. But they have done this in order that the word might be fulfilled that is written in their Law, "They hated Me without a cause."
>
> (John 15:17-25)

Verse 17 is His transition from describing His love for them to describing the world's hatred: "This I command you, that you love one another." The Greek indicates a continuous action: "Keep on loving each other." He is saying, "Devote yourselves to one another and sacrifice for one another — love each other the way I loved you."

One reason their love for each other was so important was that the world would know nothing but hatred for them. Love for each other was the only love they would ever know. In a hostile world, they desperately needed love from each other.

History shows that the apostles were hated, just as Jesus predicted. James was martyred. Paul was beheaded by Nero. Andrew persisted in preaching and was tied to a cross and crucified. Peter, too, was crucified, athough traditionally it is held that he was crucified upside down because he did not consider himself worthy of the same death as His Savior. All of them were martyred, except perhaps Matthew and also John, who was exiled to the Isle of Patmos. The rest of Christ's followers suffered persecution from the Roman government, which regarded them as disloyal citizens and a threat to the unity of the empire.

Rome was concerned about unity because the empire stretched from the Euphrates River to England and from Germany to North Africa. It included the widest variety of peoples and cultures imaginable. Such a multicultural empire could easily become divided. Worship of the emperor was seen as a way to bond the different peoples of the vast empire.

Every Roman citizen was required to worship Caesar. Once a year, he had to demonstrate his allegiance by burning a pinch of incense to the supposed deity of Caesar. Then he was required to shout, "Caesar is Lord." As long as he worshiped the emperor, he could worship any other god he wished.

But Christians would call no man Lord, so the government considered them irresponsible and disloyal and persecuted them from time to time. Mobs added to the persecution by the government. People in various parts of the empire hated the Christians because they did not fit into society.

Christians were accused of cannibalism because they talked about eating the flesh and drinking the blood of Christ at their Communion services. Some accused the Christians of immorality, thinking the Christian "love feast" was an orgy. Because Christians expected the second coming of their King, some thought they were planning a rebellion. They were suspected of arson because they said God was going to bring fire on judgment day. They were blamed for the burning of Rome in the first century.

Though the specific misunderstandings may differ, the same hostility toward Christians is true of today's world. The world does not accept Christians, because it rejects their Lord. And the world's hostility is not something we can evade without compromising. Jesus gives three reasons suffering and persecution are unavoidable for Christians.

CHRIST'S FOLLOWERS ARE NOT OF THE WORLD

First of all, Jesus' disciples are rejected by the world because they are no longer a part of the world's system. Jesus told the apostles, "If you were of the world, the world would love its own; but because you are not of the world, but I chose you out of the world, therefore the world hates you" (v. 19). They had been called out; because they were different, they no longer could fit into the world's system.

"World" is the English translation of *cosmos*, a common word in Greek. It appears often in John's writings and changes its meaning with the context. Here it means the evil, sinful system begun by Satan and acted out by men. The *cosmos* is the result and expression of human depravity. It is set against Christ, His people, and His kingdom, and it is controlled by Satan and his evil minions.

This evil world system is incapable of genuine love. When Jesus said the world loves its own, He was not saying that worldly beings love each other. "Its own" is not a masculine plural, which would indicate a love directed toward other people. The word in the Greek text is neuter plural, meaning that the people caught up in the world love their own *things*. A worldly individual loves himself and his own things. He loves others only if it is to his advantage. The world's love is always selfish, superficial, and interested only in its own advantage. It loves only if it has something to gain.

The *cosmos* is against those who love and follow Jesus, those who declare their faith in Him and show it by their words and deeds. It does not persecute those who are part of its system. Jesus said to His earthly brothers, who did not follow Him during His ministry, "The world cannot hate you; but it hates Me, because I testify of it, that its deeds are evil" (John 7:7).

People living in the world who do not know Jesus Christ are part of a system that is anti-God, anti-Christ, and satanic. That system militates against God and His principles and is opposed to all that is good, godly, and Christlike. Yet I am always amazed at how easily some Christians believe the world is tolerant of God and Jesus.

It is true that the world is religious, but religion is not the same as righteousness. False religions have a superficial tolerance of the things of God. Still, they are tools of Satan in his war against the truth. They disguise themselves with godliness, but they reveal their true nature by suppressing the truth. Throughout history, false religion has been the most aggressive opponent of the true church.

Persecution is inevitable for righteous people living in the world. Paul warned Timothy, "All who desire to live godly in Christ Jesus will be persecuted" (2 Timothy 3:12). It is an inescapable fact of godly living. But because many people who attend church are not personally antagonized, they feel the world does not oppose true Christians. It may be, however, that they get no opposition from the world because it is not obvious they are Christians.

Or perhaps they are not genuine Christians at all. The true believer stands apart from the world because he has been made holy through identification with Jesus Christ. He lives righteously and does not belong to the system. Because a genuine Christian represents God and Christ, Satan uses the world's system to attack him. That is why Jesus prayed for the Father's protection of His followers: "I do not ask Thee to take them out of the world, but to keep them from the evil one" (John 17:15).

Our lives are to be a rebuke to the sinful world. Ephesians 5:11 says, "And do not participate in the unfruitful deeds of darkness, but instead even expose them." One of the reasons we do not feel as much hatred from the world as we should is that our lives are not a rebuke. To live in a hostile and perverted world, we must be blameless. Paul, writing to the Philippian Christians, cautioned them to avoid sin, "that you may prove yourselves to be blameless and innocent, children of God above reproach in the midst of a crooked and perverse generation, among whom you appear as lights in the world" (Philippians 2:15).

Romans 1:32 describes people in the world's immoral system by saying that they not only do evil themselves but "give hearty approval" to others who do it. Some people love those who are more wicked than they because it makes them feel more righteous. When the Christian's life rebukes their sinfulness, they become hostile.

But Jesus has called us to that kind of confrontation. We cannot sit in our churches and expect non-believers to sense that they are indicted. The early church did not put up a sign saying, "Revival: All Unsaved Come in Weekdays and Feel Condemned." It should not be necessary for people to come into our church to see that we are Christians. Our lives should show it. Jesus says in Matthew 5:14 that we should be like a city that can be seen for miles because it is set on a hill. In the next verse He says that believers are like a lamp that should not be put under a basket but rather should be set on a lampstand so that it can light the entire house. Our righteousness must be visible to the world, not hidden in a church building.

We stand out from the world because Jesus has chosen us. In verse 19 He says, "I chose you out of the world." The word "chose" is in the Greek middle voice, which gives it a reflexive meaning. Jesus is saying, "I chose you *for Myself*." He has chosen us to be different. We are called to be a living rebuke to the rest of the world.

Satan does not like to lose anyone, and thus he moves to attack the child of God. Peter warns Christians, "Your adversary, the devil, prowls about like a roaring lion, seeking someone to devour" (1 Peter 5:8). Satan pursues Christians and sets the whole world in motion against them. He hates the righteous as much as he hates God, for both God and the righteous stand for the same thing.

A few years ago I participated in an intensive evangelization of a local university campus. We shared the gospel with several thousand students. The next day the college newspaper said that unless the organization sponsoring the evangelistic effort complied with university policy and discontinued its evangelistic work, "direct action [would] be taken against [it]." The dean had received complaints from students who were "accosted" and asked to enter into discussions. The dean cited campus policy that forbade using "university facilities . . . for religious conversion." In other words, students were not allowed to get saved on that campus — it was against the rules. And no amount of discussion with campus officials could get them to see the inequity of their rules.

That is an example of the way the world system resists people who want to tell the truth about sin. Anyone was free to go on that same campus and convert people to Communism. And no one objected if students organized for any other cause, no matter how bizarre. But when you told people about Jesus Christ, you broke the rules. The world does not want to be confronted with the truth.

THE WORLD HATED OUR LORD

A second reason persecution is inevitable for Christians is that the world desperately hates the Lord Jesus. Jesus said, "Remember the word that I said to you, 'A slave is not greater than his master.' If they persecuted Me, they will also persecute you; if they kept My word, they will keep yours also" (v. 20).

The Son of God loves the world, but the world hates Him. And because it hates Him, it hates those who name Him as Lord.

Not everyone rejects Christ, and not everyone will reject us. A few will listen and believe. Yet much of the world's apparent acceptance of Jesus is nothing more than a facade. Most of the movies, songs, and books about Jesus written from a secular viewpoint only confuse people by making them think they understand the truth about Jesus. But no one can really know about Jesus unless he knows something about sin and repentance.

There was a time in history when Christianity became a fad. It had survived some two centuries of intense persecution, and then, suddenly, it was accepted by the Roman government. It became the official religion of the state, and everyone wanted to be associated with Christianity. True Christianity was endangered at least as much by the shallow popularity that resulted from these developments as it had been by persecution. Because everyone was calling himself a Christian, no one understood how a Christian's life was distinctive or what Christianity stood for. Christianity had become a monstrosity, an institutionalized blasphemy, and it became unclear just what Christianity was. Satan welcomes that kind of confusion as much as he relishes persecuting the church.

There is a unique joy in being so identified with Jesus Christ that you suffer the rebuke, ridicule, and hatred directed at Him. Most Christians do not know that joy. In Philippians 3:10, Paul calls it "the fellowship of His sufferings." First Peter 2:21 says, "You have been called for this purpose, since Christ also suffered for you, leaving you an example for you to follow in His steps." But when we share His sufferings, we also share His joy over those who come to God. And that makes all the sacrifices worthwhile.

THE WORLD DOES NOT KNOW GOD

In verse 21, Jesus tells the disciples another reason persecution must come: "But all these things they will do to you for My name's sake, because they do not know the One who sent Me." The Jews of Jesus' day prided themselves on what they thought was an in-depth knowledge of God. When Jesus said that they did not know God, the religious leaders were infuriated. But in rejecting Christ they themselves proved that He was right. They claimed to know God, yet they hated Christ, who was God in human flesh. Their love for God was a facade.

What many people fail to realize is that religion itself is perhaps the greatest hindrance to the knowledge of the true God. The world's approach to religion is to postulate a god and worship him, even though that god does not exist outside man's imagination. Jesus exposed the false religion propounded by the Jewish leaders when He said, "You are of your father the devil, and you want to do the desires of your father" (John 8:44).

The problem is not that men have no access to the truth about God. Romans 1:19 says, "That which is known about God is evident within them; for God made it evident to them." God gives everyone basic knowledge that He exists through both innate knowledge and nature. People willfully reject the truth, not because of ignorance but because they love the darkness rather than the light. Exposing men to the truth is like shining a light on an insect — the bug just wants to crawl back into the darkness.

God gave the Jews of Jesus' day the Old Testament and Jesus Christ. They heard what Christ said and saw what He did. But they only killed Him. They rejected everything God could reveal to them. It was the one sin for which there could be no remedy. After seeing Him cast out a demon, a group of Pharisees said, "This man casts out demons only by Beelzebul the ruler of the demons" (Matthew 12:24). Their rejection of Him was complete and irreversible. They were rejecting the fullest possible revelation.

Jesus warns them in Matthew 12:31, "Any sin and blasphemy shall be forgiven men, but blasphemy against the Spirit shall not be forgiven." He had done everything through the Holy Spirit. In rejecting Him and attributing His works to Satan's power, they were blaspheming the Spirit. They could not be forgiven because they had rejected full revelation. There was nothing more they could see or hear that would change their rejection.

Jesus quotes Psalms 35:19 and 69:4 in verse 25 of John 15: "They hated Me without a cause." There was no reason for them to reject Christ. Their rejection of Him was a fulfillment of David's words. That does not mean God planned that they would hate Jesus; He planned that their hatred of Him would be completely *without cause*. Jesus had healed all manner of diseases; He had fed multitudes; He had been completely sinless. There was no reason for anyone to hate Him.

The world hated Jesus because He exposed its sin. When His divine holiness shone on those of the world, it revealed their love of darkness. Instead of turning to Him in faith and love, they turned against Him in hatred.

The world is no different today — it still hates Jesus. And it still hates those who truly serve Him. If you are going to follow Him, you will have to suffer the hatred of the world. If you are unwilling, you cannot be His disciple. The price may seem high, but the rewards are higher.

Suffering for Christ's sake is the calling of every believer (2 Timothy 3:12). He does not call any of us to a life without suffering or persecution. Suffering is a part of the cost everyone must count if he wants to be a disciple.

Still, to be persecuted for Him is a unique privilege. It is a special joy to be identified with Christ in His suffering (Philippians 3:10). And when we truly suffer for righteousness' sake — when we are willing to be hated without a cause — that will be when we begin to understand persecution not as a thing to be resisted or avoided but as a wonderful aspect of our fellowship with Christ.

Conclusion

The ministry of Jesus among the mass of men was over in John 12. From John 13 through John 16 His ministry was uniquely to His disciples. That ministry occurred in a brief period of hours, the night before His crucifixion, and in one place, the upper room. During those hours Jesus gave His disciples — and, consequently, all believers throughout history — His last will and testament — His legacy. It is the inheritance of every believer in Christ.

It has been our privilege to look into that legacy. But we have only scratched the surface of a portion of the rich promise contained in just three chapters of our Lord's final discourse. You can easily see that a lifetime of study still might not plumb the depths of all that He left as His legacy. Look again at all He gave:

He gave the proof of His love. "Jesus . . . rose from supper, and laid aside His garments; and taking a towel, He girded Himself about. Then He poured water into the basin, and began to wash the disciples' feet, and to wipe them with the towel with which He was girded" (13:3-5). Later, Peter and the rest of the disciples would know Christ's love through His death. But in the upper room they saw a glimpse of it through Jesus' washing of their feet.

He gave the hope of heaven. "Let not your heart be troubled; believe in God, believe also in Me. In My Father's house are many dwelling places; if it were not so, I would have told you; for I go to prepare a place for you. And if I go to prepare a place for you, I will come again, and receive you to Myself; that where I am you may be also" (14:1-3). In those days in Israel, when a son married, a new apartment was added onto the father's house. Generation after generation of the extended family lived together in one home. That is how heaven is. We are all to be in the Father's house. Jesus is preparing our rooms.

He gave the guarantee of power. "Truly, truly, I say to you, he who believes in Me, the works that I do shall he do also; and greater works than these shall he do; because I go to the Father" (14:12). Jesus did not mean that the disciples would do works that were greater than His in quality or type, but that they would do works that were greater in extent. During Christ's ministry on earth He faced mostly rejection, and He never left the tiny land of Palestine. But on the day of Pentecost, the Spirit of God came, and the apostles started preaching — and revolutionized Jerusalem. Later, when persecution came to the Christians in Jerusalem, they scattered throughout Samaria and Judea, preaching the gospel as they went. Then the apostle Paul and his associates spread the gospel to many more lands. That process is still going on today.

He gave the assurance of supply. "And whatever you ask in My name, that will I do, that the Father may be glorified in the Son. If you ask Me anything in My name, I will do it" (14:13-14). To pray in His name is to bring requests before God that are consistent with who He is. Prayer is not for us to get what we want, and it is not to change God from doing what He is going to do anyway. Prayer is to give God the opportunity to show Himself so that we can praise Him for what He is doing.

He gave the gift of the Spirit. "And I will ask the Father, and He will give you another Helper, that He may be with you forever; that is the Spirit of truth" (14:16-17a). Jesus promised a supernatural Helper, or Comforter, of the exact same kind as He. This Comforter is the Holy Spirit, the Spirit of Christ. He lives within Christ's disciples, not just near them. He empowers them and convicts those to whom they preach. His ministry is to "convict the world of sin, because they believe not on me; of righteousness, because I go to my Father, and ye see me no more; of judgment, because the prince of this world is judged" (16:9-11, KJV).

He gave the possession of divine truth, the Word of God. "But the Helper, the Holy Spirit, whom the Father will send in My name He will teach you all things, and bring to your remembrance all that I said to you" (14:26). This promise had a primary application to the writers of the New Testament, the apostolic preachers in the early era of the church. It was a promise of verbal inspiration. The Holy Spirit would bring to their remembrance all that Jesus had taught them, and He would give them further teaching through the years as they served Him. The Bible is accurate, for the Holy Spirit never lies. There is no lie in Him; He is the "Spirit of truth" (John 14:17; 15:26; 16:13).

He gave the promise of peace. "Peace I leave with you: My peace I give to you; not as the world gives, do I give to you. Let not your heart be troubled, nor let it be fearful" (14:27). One kind of peace in Scripture is peace *with* God. That is the objective peace of relationship with Him. But there is also the subjective peace of tranquility of mind, the peace *of* God. "The Lord is near," Paul writes in Philippians 4:5. But that is not a reference to the second coming. It is a reference to the presence of the Lord in our lives today. Because He is at hand, we should be "anxious for nothing" (Philippians 4:6).

He gave the promise of fruit. "I am the vine; you are the branches; he that abides in Me, and I in him, he bears much fruit; for apart from Me you can do nothing" (15:5). Fruit is the product of a life that has continuing life. It lives beyond us; it is something we reproduce. Christians are part of a product that will go throughout eternity like ripples in an everlasting pond. We have lives that will reverberate through all the corridors of heaven forever and ever.

He gave the promise of the pain of persecution. "If the world hates you, you know that it has hated me before it hated you. If you were of the world, the world would love its own; but because you are not of the world, but I chose you out of the world, therefore the world hates you" (15:18-19). The servant is not greater than his Lord. The world hates and rejects the message of sin. Christ unmasks the world and reveals its sin. So the world hates Him, and it hates us. Jesus warned His disciples, "These things I have spoken to you, that you may be kept from stumbling" (16:1).

He gave the promise of joy. "These things I have spoken to you, that My joy may be in you and that your joy may be made full" (15:11). Joy is the result of everything Jesus has said, everything He has given us. A woman has agony when she is in labor, but when she is delivered of a child, she remembers her pain no more. Believers will have sorrow and painful circumstances, but out of those very circumstances will come the greatest joy. Jesus says, "I will see you again, and your heart will rejoice, and no one takes your joy away from you" (16:22*b*).

What a legacy! The proof of love, hope of heaven, power, supply, the Holy Spirit, truth, peace, fruitfulness, persecution, and joy. All of these things are ours, because He is ours. Hear His gracious words: "I will not leave you as orphans; I will come to you. After a

little while the world will behold Me no more; but you will behold
Me; because I live, you shall live also. In that day you shall know
that I am in My Father, and you in Me, and I in you" (14:18-20). Jesus was going away in physical form, but He was going to be with
the disciples in spiritual form. Even today, He dwells in every single
believer with His own marvelous presence. This legacy is yours if
you believe.